THE THIRTEEN
PETALLED ROSE

for Z.
from G

w/ goodness
&
wishes

Brillo Colley
2018

THE THIRTEEN PETALLED ROSE

*A Discourse on the Essence
of Jewish Existence and Belief*

Adin Steinsaltz

Translated by
Yehuda Hanegbi

A Member of the Perseus Books Group
New York

Chapter 8 of this book appeared originally in the *Shefa Quarterly*

Books published by Basic Books are available at special discounts for bulk purchases in the United States by corporations, institutions, and other organizations. For more information, please contact the Special Markets Department at the Perseus Books Group, 11 Cambridge Center, Cambridge MA 02142, or call (617) 252-5298, (800) 255-1514, or e-mail special.markets@perseusbooks.com.

Library of Congress Cataloging-in-Publication Data
  Steinsaltz, Adin.
  [Sheloshah 'asar 'ale ha-shoshanah. English]
  The thirteen petalled rose : a discourse on the essence of Jewish existence and belief / Adin Steinsaltz ; translated by Yehuda Hanegbi. — [Expanded ed.]
      p. cm.
  "Chapter 8 of this book appeared originally in the Shefa Quarterly."
  ISBN-13: 978-0-465-08272-8(alk. paper)
  ISBN-10: 0-465-08272-6 (alk. paper)
  1. Cabala. 2. Judaism. I. Title.

BM525.S7413 2006
296.3—dc22

2006022491

CONTENTS

"As the rose among the thorns, so is my love among the maidens." (Song of Songs 2:2)

What is the rose—it is Knesset Yisrael, the Community of Israel. For there is a rose (above) and a rose (below). Just as the rose, which is among the thorns has red and white, so does Knesset Yisrael have justice and mercy. Just as a rose has thirteen petals, so does Knesset Yisrael have thirteen measures of compassion encompassing it on all its sides.

. . . Five strong petals surround the rose, and these five, called salvations, are five gates. Concerning which secret it is written: "I will lift up the cup of salvation." (Psalms 116:13)

OPENING LINES OF THE ZOHAR

PREFACE TO THE
THIRTEEN PETALLED ROSE

I WROTE THIS BOOK many years ago to provide answers to ten important questions that are the theoretical and spiritual basis for Jewish life.

Writing this book was an extraordinary experience for me. It was written or dictated in a lonely room with no understanding or imagining of who the readers would be. At first, I did not know if there would be any readers for this book. Parts of it seemed too complicated; parts of it seemed very, very distant from anyone's way of thinking.

Over the years, somehow, *The Thirteen Petalled Rose* has had a powerful impact on a great number of people. I came to understand the book's effect during those small encounters that an author has with his readers. In some cases, the impact was so compelling that it was surely beyond my wildest expectations. At least for some individuals, the encounter with this book was a beginning of a change in their lives; for some people, a drastic change of behavior.

There is no real way to explain this, except for perhaps two small points. First, the *Rose* cannot be counted among the great number of books written *about* kabbalah. In its humble way, and without using very technical terms, it is a small, insufficiently clear book *of* kabbalah. The book's great advantage is that it is not an outsider's point of view; rather, it is a glimpse of the inside. And it seems that looking into the inside of Jewish life, of Jewish thinking, had and has a great influence on people.

Second, I wrote this book in a way that, at least, I think is true. To my mind, kabbalah is the theology of the Jewish people. The *Rose* is not so much about what others have to say about kabbalah. The book describes what I think is the true picture of kabbalah, in most of its forms otherwise so hidden. The kabbalah is hidden, not just by language, but by a very difficult style, by a myriad of almost incomprehensible formulas. This is an attempt not to vulgarize any of them, but to restate some of the principles of kabbalah, which seem to me to be true.

In our time, when some forms of distorted, commercialized and cheap kinds of kabbalah have become fashionable, it has to be specifically mentioned that this book does not attempt to make kabbalah especially popular. This is a book that people have to encounter; it does not really reach out to everybody. The reader must make his own effort and at least that effort is, for many people, a touch upon the print of truth—which is of extraordinary power.

Although *The Thirteen Petalled Rose* was originally written in Hebrew, it was only many years after its publication in several other languages that it finally appeared in its original form. At that time, a number of well-meaning people wanted to correct, to perfect the original text. However, after some years, they decided to leave it as it was. Two new chapters were added and endnotes to the Hebrew text were compiled. The interested reader is referred to the Hebrew edition for the endnotes.

The biggest change from the original English edition to this reissued version is the inclusion here of the two chapters that had been added to the Hebrew version. They are very different from each other and from the rest of the chapters. One is a prolonged essay on the ways of prayer, not on the forms, but on the way that people do pray. The other is a commentary on an excerpt from the Zohar, the very basic book of kabbalah, which contains its key notions. The explanation is given in a way that the reader encounters something authentic, something of the thing in itself—not writing about it, not around it, but the thing as it is.

For this edition, I recall fondly the memory of my late friend Yehuda Hanegbi. He was the one who originally posed those original questions to me, urged me to give the answers, and took the trouble of translating them into English.

The Rose reveals a little bit of that thing which is the mystery of what one calls truth. It is sometimes not elaborate. It sometimes does not seem especially spiritual. It sometimes does not appear to be especially innovative. Yet it has its own beauty. *The Thirteen Petalled Rose* is offered to readers so that they can try to encounter something which is true, in itself. For that purpose, the meeting between book and reader may be of use.

ADIN STEINSALTZ

Jerusalem
March 2006

THE THIRTEEN
PETALLED ROSE

1

Worlds

THE PHYSICAL WORLD in which we live, the objectively observed universe around us, is only a part of an inconceivably vast system of worlds. Most of these worlds are spiritual in their essence; they are of a different order from our known world. Which does not necessarily mean that they exist somewhere else, but means rather that they exist in different dimensions of being. What is more, the various worlds interpenetrate and interact in such a way that they can be considered counterparts of one another, each reflecting or projecting itself on the one below or above it, with all the modifications, changes, and even distortions that are the result of such interaction. It is the sum of this infinitely complex exchange of influence back and forth among different domains that comprises the specific world of reality we experience in our everyday life.

In speaking of higher or lower worlds, I do not mean to describe an actual physical relation; for in the realm of the spiritual there is no such division, and the words "high" and "low" refer only to the place of any particular world on the ladder of causality. To call a world higher signifies that it is more primary, more basic in terms of being close to a primal source of influence; while a lower world would be a secondary world—in a sense, a copy. Yet the copy is not just an imitation but rather a whole system, with a more or less independent life of its own, its own variety of experience, characteristics, and properties.

The world in which we ordinarily live, with all that it embraces, is called the "world of action"; and it includes the world of both our sensual and our nonsensual apprehension. But this world of action itself is not all of the same essence and the same quality. The lower part of the world of action is what is known as the "world of physical nature" and of more or less mechanical processes—that is to say, the world where natural law prevails; while above this world of physical nature is another part of the same world which we may call the "world of spiritual action." What is common to these two domains of the world of action is man, the human creature so situated between them that he partakes of both. As a part of the physical system of the universe, man is subordinate to the physical, chemical, and biological laws of nature; while from the standpoint of his consciousness, even when this consciousness is totally occupied with matters of a lower order, man belongs to the spiritual world, the world of ideas. To be sure, these ideas of the world of action are almost completely bound up with the material world, growing out of it and reaching farther, but never really getting out of it; and this is as true for the heights of the most far-reaching and encompassing philosophy as it is for the thought processes of the ignorant person, the primitive savage, or the child.

Every aspect of human existence is therefore made up of both matter and spirit. And at the same time, in the world of action the spiritual is subordinate to the material, in keeping with the fact that the laws of nature determine the face and form of all things and serve as focal points for all processes. In this world the spirit can appear and perform its role only on the solid basis of the workings of what we call the "forces of nature." In other words, no matter how abstract or divorced it is from so-called reality, thought still belongs to the world of action.

The world of action, however, is only one world in a general system of four fundamental dimensions of being, or four different worlds, each with its own cosmos of varying essences. These four worlds have been called, in order from the highest to the lowest, "emanation," "creation," "formation," and "action." Thus, the world directly above ours is the world of formation. To understand the difference, one must first understand certain factors common to all four worlds. These factors were traditionally known as "world," "year," and "soul"; nowadays we would call them "space," "time," and "self" (experience of one's being). Each world is distinguished from the others by the way these three factors are manifested in it. For example, in our world, physical place is a necessary external element for the existence of things; it is the background against which all objects move and all creatures function. In the higher worlds, and also in the world of spiritual action, that which is analogous to space in the world of physical action is called a "mansion." It is the framework within which various forms and beings converge and connect. Perhaps one may compare it to those self-contained systems—known in mathematics as "groups" or "fields"—in each of which all the unit parts are related in a definite way to the other parts and to the whole. Such systems may be inhabited or full to capacity, or they may be relatively sparse or empty. Whatever the case, such a system of related existences constitutes a "place" in the abstract—a "mansion" in the higher worlds.

Time also has a different significance in the other worlds. In our domain of experience, time is measured by the movement of physical objects in space. The "year" as it is called abstractly constitutes the very process of change; it is the passage from one thing to another, from form to form, and it also includes within itself the concept of causality as that which keeps all transition from form to form within the bounds of law. Indeed, upon ascending the order of worlds, this time system becomes increasingly abstract and less and less representative of anything that we know as time in the physical world; it becomes no more than the purest essence of change, or even of the possibility of potential change.

Finally, what we call "soul" is, in the physical dimension, the totality of living creatures functioning in the time and space dimensions of this world. Although they are an essential part of this world, they are distinguished from the general background by their self-consciousness and knowledge of this world. Similarly, in the higher world, the souls are self-conscious essences acting within the framework of the mansion and the year of their world.

THE WORLD OF FORMATION may be said to be, in its essence, a world of feeling. It is a world whose main substance, or type of experience, is emotion of one kind or another, and in which such emotions are the elements that determine its patterns. The living beings in it are conscious manifestations of particular impulses—impulses to perform one or another act or respond in one or another way—or of the power to carry through an incentive, to realize, to fulfill the tendency of an inclination or an inspiration. The living creatures of the world of formation, the beings who function in it as we function in the world of action, are called, in a general way, "angels."

An angel is a spiritual reality with its own unique content, qualities, and character. What distinguishes one angel from another is not the physical quality of spatial apartness but difference of level—one being above or below another—with respect to fundamental causality in terms of some difference in essence. Now as we have said, angels are beings in the world that is the domain of emotion and feeling; and since this is the case, the substantial quality of an angel may be an impulse or a drive—say, an inclination in the direction of love or a seizure of fear, or pity, or the like. To express a larger totality of being, something more comprehensive, we may refer to "a camp of angels." In the general camp of love, for example, there are many subdivisions, virtually innumerable shades and gradations of tender feeling. No two loves are alike in emotion, just as no two ideas are alike. Thus, any general and inclusive drive or impulse is a whole camp, perhaps even a mansion, and is not consistently the same at every level. Whereas among human beings emotions change and vary either as persons change or according to the circumstances of time and place, an angel is totally the manifestation of a single emotional essence. The essence of an angel, therefore, is defined by the limits of a particular emotion, in terms of itself, just as personality and inwardness define the self of each person in our world. An angel, however, is not merely a fragment of existence doing nothing more than just manifesting an emotion; it is a whole and integral being, conscious of itself and its surroundings and able to act and create and do things within the framework of the world of formation. The nature of the angel is to be, to a degree, as its name in Hebrew signifies, a messenger, to constitute a permanent contact between our world of action and the higher worlds. The angel is the one who effects transfers of the vital plenty between worlds. An angel's missions go in two directions: it may serve as an emissary of God downward, to other angels and to worlds and creatures below the world of formation; and it may also serve as the one who carries things upwards from below, from our world to the higher worlds.

The real difference between man and angel is not the fact that man has a body, because the essential comparison is between the human *soul* and the angel. The soul of man is most complex and includes a whole world of different existential elements of all kinds, while the angel is a being of single essence and therefore in a sense one-dimensional. In addition, man—because of his many-sidedness, his capacity to contain contradictions, and his gift of an inner power of soul, that divine spark that makes him man—has the capacity to distinguish between one thing and another, especially between good and evil. It is this capacity which makes it possible for him to rise to great heights, and by the same token creates the possibility for his failure and backsliding, neither of which is true for the angel. From the point of view of its essence, the angel is eternally the same; it is static, an unchanging existence, whether temporary or eternal, fixed within the rigid limits of quality given at its very creation.

Among the many thousands of angels to be found in the various worlds are those that have existed from the very beginning of time, for they are an unaltering part of the Eternal Being and the fixed order of the universe. These angels in a sense constitute the channels of plenty through which the divine grace rises and descends in the worlds.

But there are also angels that are continuously being created anew, in all the worlds, and especially in the world of action where thoughts, deeds, and experiences give rise to angels of different kinds. Every *mitzvah* that a man does is not only an act of transformation in the material world; it is also a spiritual act, sacred in itself. And this aspect of concentrated spirituality and holiness in the *mitzvah* is the chief component of that which becomes an angel. In other words, the emotion, the intention, the essential holiness of the act combine to become the essence of the *mitzvah* as an existence in itself, as something that has objective reality. And this separate existence of the *mitzvah*, by being unique and holy, creates the angel, a new spiritual reality that belongs to the world of formation. So it is that the act of performing a *mitzvah* extends beyond its effect in the material world and, by the power of the spiritual holiness within it—holiness in direct communion with all the upper worlds—causes a primary and significant transformation.

More precisely, the person who performs a *mitzvah*, who prays or directs his mind toward the Divine, in so doing creates an angel, which is a sort of reaching out on the part of man to the higher worlds. Such an angel, however, connected in its essence to the man who created it, still lives, on the whole, in a different dimension of being, namely in the world of formation. And it is in this world of formation that the *mitzvah* acquires substance. This is the process by which the specific message or offering to God that is intrinsic in the *mitzvah* rises upward and introduces changes in the system of the higher worlds—foremost in the world of formation. From here, in turn, they influence the worlds above them. So we see that a supreme act is performed when what is done below becomes detached from particular physical place, time, and person and becomes an angel.

Conversely, an angel is sometimes sent downward from a higher world to a lower. For what we call the mission of the angel can be manifested in many different ways. The angel cannot reveal its true form to man, whose being, senses, and instruments of perception belong only to the world of action: in the world of action there are no means of grasping the angel. It continues to belong to a different dimension even when apprehended in one form or another. This may be compared with those frequencies of an electromagnetic field that are beyond the limited range ordinarily perceived by our senses. We know that human vision assimilates only a small fragment of the spectrum; as far as our senses are concerned, the rest of it does not exist. That which is ordinarily invisible is "seen" only through appropriate instruments of transmutation, or interpretation, when, in the language of the Kabbalah, they are dressed in the clothes or vessels that make it possible for us to apprehend them—as, for example, radio or television waves have to be transmitted through appropriate vessels to be revealed to our senses. In the same way, there are aspects of the reality of the spiritual world of which we are only vaguely conscious. Even animals can sometimes be sensitive, if to a limited degree, to the presence of such a spiritual essence. The ass of Balaam, for instance, who "saw" an angel, did not of course actually see an angel: probably the animal had some obscure sensation of being confronted or threatened by something.

Angels have been revealed to human beings in either of two ways: one is through the vision of the prophet, the seer, or the holy man—that is, an experience by a person on the highest level; the other is through an isolated act of apprehension by an ordinary person suddenly privileged to receive a revelation of things from higher levels. And even so, when such a person or prophet does in some way experience the reality of an angel, his perception, limited by his senses, remains bound to material structures, and his language inevitably tends to expressions of actual or imagined physical forms. Thus, when the prophet tries to describe or to explain to others his experience of seeing an angel, the description verges on the eerie and fantastic. Terms like "winged creature of heaven" or "eyes of the supreme chariot" can be only a pale and inadequate representation of the experience because this experience belongs to another realm with another system of imagery. The description will of necessity tend to be anthropomorphic. Or when, as we know, the angel whom the prophet describes as having the face of an ox does not have any face at all—and certainly not that of an ox—its inner essence, seeking elucidation and reflection within material reality, may express itself in a way that shows a certain likeness between the face of an angel and the face of an ox as the expression of a known spiritual quality.

Thus, all the articulated visions of prophecy are nothing more than ways of representing an abstract formless spiritual reality in the vocabulary of human language; although, to be sure, there may also be a revelation of an angel in quite ordinary form, clothed in some familiar vessel and manifested as a "normal" phenomenon in nature. The difficulty is that the one who sees an angel in this way does not always know that it is an apparition, that the pillar of fire or the image of a man does not belong entirely to the realm of natural cause and effect. And at the same time, the angel—that is to say, the force sent from a higher world—makes its appearance and to a certain extent acts in the material world, being either entirely subject to the laws of our world or operating in a sort of vacuum between the worlds in which physical nature is no more than a kind of garment for some higher substance. In the Bible, Manoah, the father of Samson, sees the angel in the image of a prophet; yet he senses in some inexplicable way that it is not a man he sees, that he is witnessing a phenomenon of a different order. Only when the angel changes form completely and becomes a pillar of fire does Manoah recognize that this being, this marvel which he has seen and with whom he has conversed, was not a man, not a prophet, but a being from another dimension of reality—that is to say, an angel.

The creation of an angel in our world and the immediate relegation of this angel to another world is, in itself, not at all a supernatural phenomenon; it is a part of a familiar realm of experience, an integral piece of life, which may even seem ordinary and commonplace because of its traditional rootedness in the system of *mitzvot,* or the order of sanctity. When we are in the act of creating the angel, we have no perception of the angel being created, and this act seems to be a part of the whole structure of the practical material world in which we live. Similarly, the angel who is sent to us from another world does not always have a significance or impact beyond the normal laws of physical nature. Indeed, it often happens that the angel precisely reveals itself in nature, in the ordinary common-sense world of causality, and only a prophetic insight or divination can show when, and to what extent, it is the work of higher forces. For man by his very nature is bound to the system of higher worlds, even though ordinarily this system is not revealed and known to him. As a result, the system of higher worlds seems to him to be natural, just as the whole of his two-sided existence, including both matter and spirit, seems self-evident to him. Man does not wonder at all about those passages he goes through all the time in the world of action, from the realm of material existence to the realm of spiritual existence. What is more, the rest of the other worlds that also penetrate our world may appear to us as part of something quite natural. It may be said that the realities of the angel and of the world of formation are part of a system of "natural" being which is as bound by law as that aspect of existence we are able to observe directly. Therefore neither the existence of the angel nor his "mission," taking him from world to world, need break through the reality of nature in the broadest sense of the word.

The domain of angels, the world of formation, is a general system of nonphysical essences, most of them quite simple and consistent in their being. Each angel has a well-defined character which is manifested in the way it functions in our world. This is why it is said that an angel can carry out only one mission, for the essence of an angel is beyond the existing many-sidedness of man. The particular essence of an angel can be evinced in terms of different things and separate forms, but it remains a single thing in itself, like a simple force of nature. Because even though the angel is a being that possesses divine consciousness, its specific essence and function are not altered by it, just as physical forces in the world are specific and single in their mode of functioning and do not keep changing their essences. It follows, then, that just as there are holy angels, built into and created by the sacred system, there are also destructive angels, called "devils" or "demons," who are the emanations of the connection of man with those aspects of reality which are the opposite of holiness. Here, too, the actions of man and his modes of existence, in all their forms, create angels, but angels of another sort, from another level and a different reality. These are hostile angels that may be part of a lower world or even of a higher, more spiritual world—this last because even though they do not belong to the realm of holiness, as in all worlds and systems of being, there is a mutual interpenetration and influence between the holy and the not-holy.

IMMEDIATELY ABOVE the world of formation is the world called the "world of creation," which, like the others, includes many different realms, levels, and mansions. And just as the world of formation is comprised of a multitude of spiritual beings whose essence is pure feeling and emotion, the world of creation is a world of pure mind. This mind quality of the world of creation is not a merely intellectual essence but rather expresses itself as the power and capacity to grasp things with a genuine, inner understanding; it is, in other words, the mind as creator as well as that which registers and absorbs knowledge.

One of the other names for the world of creation is "world of the throne," taken from Ezekiel's vision of the divine "throne of glory." On the whole, however, that aspect of the Divine that is revealed to the prophets is the world directly above the world of creation known as the "world of emanation." This is the source from which God is made known to a few, while the world of creation is His seat or His throne, from which, as it is written, "the earth is His footstool." Moreover, the Divine Throne or Chariot is the means through which the divine plenty descends to the creatures and things of our world and makes contact with the many complex systems of all the worlds. So that the world of creation is also the crossroads of existence. It is the focal point at which the plenty rising from the lower worlds and the plenty descending from the higher worlds meet and enter into some sort of relation with each other. Hence an understanding of the "way of the Chariot"—that is, an understanding of the way the Divine Throne of Glory operates—is the highest secret of the esoteric doctrine. And beyond this secret a human being, even a man of vision or one who has a revelation, can receive only uncertain impressions of such essences as are structurally beyond human comprehension. For the world of creation is a world which man has been able to reach only at the very highest point of his development, demonstrating in this way that part of his soul belongs to the special realm. So it is that for someone to comprehend the secret of the Chariot means that he is standing at the very focal point of the intersection of different worlds. At this intersection he is given knowledge of all existence and transformation, past, present, and future, and is aware of the Divine as prime cause and mover of all the forces acting from every direction. Obviously, it is impossible for man as man to achieve such comprehension completely; nevertheless, even partial insight into the Chariot provides one with a sense of what is happening in all the worlds.

In the world of creation, too, there are mansions—that is to say, places in the metaphysical sense, spheres of being within which there is a certain measured rhythm of time, in one form or another, with a relation between past, present, and future, between cause and effect, and in which there are souls and creatures who belong specifically to this world. These creatures of the world of creation, the living souls in it, are the higher angels called "seraphs." Like the angels of the world of formation, the seraphs are singular abstract essences, not given to change. But whereas the angels of the world of formation are embodiments of pure emotion, those of the world of creation are essences of pure intelligence. The seraphs are angels who manifest the higher levels of mind. They also reflect the differences among various planes of consciousness and comprehension, in itself a particular aspect of mind. Finally, every such creature of the world of creation also serves as an angel-messenger, receiving the plenty from the angelic beings and the souls of the world of formation, and raising them up to a higher level in the world of creation and further, to endless heights.

The ascendancy of the world of creation over the world of formation is not only a matter of the superiority of mind and consciousness over the emotions; it also lies in the fact that the world of creation itself is a "higher" world: in the sense that the various worlds are characterized as higher or lower in relation to the degree of their transparency to the divine light, which is their very light and substance. As one descends in the system of worlds, materiality becomes ever greater: in other words, the beings of the lower worlds feel their independent existence with greater intensity than the beings of the higher; they are more aware of being separate individual selves. And this consciousness of their separate selfdom blocks the divine plenty and at the same time obscures the truly unchanging essence that lurks beneath the individual personality. In short, the lower the world, the more it is pervaded by a sense of the "I," and consequently the more it is subject to the obscuring of the divine essence. It can be said, however, that all of the worlds—and, indeed, any separate realms of being—exist only by virtue of the fact that God makes Himself hidden. For when the divine plenty is manifested in its complete fullness there is no room for the existence of anything else. A world can exist only as a result of the concealment of its Creator. As one descends from higher worlds to lower, with each new level of descent the separateness, the independence of the world from it becomes more pronounced and emphatic, while the divine plenty becomes more hidden. Hence the creatures in the world of action may reach (as men often do) a condition in which they are not only unaware of the life-giving divine plenty, but may even repudiate its existence altogether. On the other hand, as one ascends the scale of being, the worlds become ever more clear and transparent to the divine plenty.

If in our world one needs prophetic insight or an opening of faith to distinguish the divine plenty in all its variety of form and on all its levels, in the higher worlds everything is more lucid and offers less resistance to the divine plenty. So that in being above the other two worlds—of action and formation—the world of creation is also more translucently clear, its creatures are more fully cognizant of the manner in which their world is constantly being created as one or another manifestation of the divine plenty. At the same time, since the world of creation is still a separate world, its creatures and souls have their own individual selves. They may indeed perceive the divine light, and they may fully accept its dominance in everything. Nevertheless, in feeling themselves separate from this light, they recognize their independent existence. Which is to say that even the seraph yearns mightily to approach the Divine, for despite his being so far above anything man can grasp, and despite his being the embodiment of understanding and higher intelligence, he is aware that his is a reality still disconnected from the Divine.

In fact, only beyond the world of creation, in the world of emanation, the highest of worlds, which is in a sense no longer really a world, can one speak of such absolute clarity and transparency that no concealment of any essence whatsoever is possible, and that consequently essences do not exhibit any particular separate self at all. Only in the world of emanation is there no hiding of the revealed divinity by every fence or screen that sets things apart. This is why one may say that the world of emanation is no longer a world, but is itself the Godhead. The world of creation is, for all its excellences and purity, still an independent existence with its own personality, its "I" as distinct from the divine being. The difference between the world of emanation and the world of creation is thus greater than that between any other two levels. It is the edge of the whole system of independent existences, each one divided from the other by "screens," and beyond it is the source of all being, where there are no such screens anymore.

An archetypal representation of a "screen" is the curtain dividing the humanly sacred from the Holy of Holies in the Holy Temple. For the Holy Temple is, in a sense, a symbolic model of the whole system of the worlds. A screen is thus something that acts as a barrier to the free flow of the divine plenty in all its purity; it is that which brings about a certain obscuring and modification of its light. For so long as the divine light passes through levels and planes that are transparent, there may be an alteration of color, or of form, or of the quality of the revelation, but the light itself remains essentially light. But what happens when the light strikes against a screen? Even though the light may be discerned on the dark side of the screen as a result of some "enlightenment," on the other side, the light itself does not penetrate.

This idea of a screen is only an image to explain the essence of the differences among all things. In the world of emanation, in the Godhead, there are no such barriers and the unity is complete. In order for a world to exist separate from the Godhead, there has to be a contraction of the highest essence. This contraction of infinite wisdom, or withdrawal of divine plenty, is therefore the basis for the creation of the universe; and the screen—representing the hiddenness of the Divine—is the basis for making the worlds manifest as separate worlds. This is the central imagery of Genesis: in the beginning was concealment and withdrawal—"darkness on the face of the deep." And out of this darkness, which follows from the existence of the screen, the mold of a world, which will be the world itself, can be imprinted.

As FOR OUR WORLD—the world of action—besides a physical world, it also contains a spiritual world—in fact, a rather large number of spiritual worlds. These worlds and their various mansions vary, greatly—indeed, so greatly that it is extremely difficult to see any unity in their spiritual significance. On the one hand, those domains of the spirit that issue from wisdom and creativity—such as philosophy, mathematics, art, poetry, and the like, which are morally or qualitatively neutral in their ideas of truth or beauty—are readily recognizable. On the other hand, there are domains of the spirit that have a certain Gnostic significance, with a different value system, and that thus lend themselves to either a positive or a negative spirituality. For just as there is room for both physical and spiritual functioning of all kinds that raise the world and man to higher levels of holiness in the world of action, so there is also that which makes contact between the world of human beings and those worlds lower than ours. These worlds are called the "realms of evil," the worlds of the *kelipah,* the outer shell.

The domains of the Kelipah constitute mansions, and in them, too, there are hierarchical systems, one above the other (actually one beneath the other), with the evil becoming more emphatic and more obvious with each distinct level. And, as may be surmised, there is a strong interrelation with the world of action. For although in itself the world of action is neutral, in terms of its Gnostic implication it belongs to the worlds of evil, to one of the levels of the outer shell called *Kelipah Noga*. This is a level of being containing all that is not in its essence directed either toward or against holiness. In terms of holiness, then, it holds a neutral position. Nevertheless, when man sinks into this neutral position entirely, without disentangling himself at all from it, he fails to realize his specific human destiny and is found wanting in the very core of his being.

Beneath the domain of *Kelipah Noga* are the thoroughly evil worlds. Each one of them has its own aspect of evil and, as is the case with the worlds of holiness, is dynamically connected to the others, by the bonds of transformation between worlds and planes, in a process that continues down to the very lowest depth of evil. As in all the worlds, so in the realms of evil, manifestation takes three forms: worlds, year, and soul. In other words, there is a general background of existence, acting as place in the spiritual sense (world); there is an aspect connected with the relation to time and causality (year); and likewise they have a soul aspect—that is, spiritual creatures inhabiting the worlds of evil. Those beings inhabiting the worlds of evil are also called "angels," but they are rather subversive angels, angels of destruction. And like the angels of the higher worlds, they are also spiritual beings and are limited each to a well-defined essence and each to its own purpose. Just as there is in the domain of holiness the quality (or angel) of love-in-holiness, of awe-in-holiness, and the like, so there are contrasting emanations and impulses in the domain of evil, angels of destruction expressing love-in-wickedness, fear-in-corruption, and the like.

Some of these pernicious angels are self-sufficient beings with clearly defined and specific characters, whose existence is, in a certain sense, eternal—at least until such time as evil will vanish from the face of the earth. In addition, there are the subversive angels created by the actions of men, by the objectification of malevolence: the evil thought, the hate-inspired wish, the wicked deed. For beside its visibly destructive consequences, every act of malice or evil creates an abstract Gnostic being, who is a bad angel, an angel belonging to the plane of evil corresponding to the state of mind that brought it into being. In their inner essence, however, the creatures of realms of evil are not independent entities living by their own forces; their existence is contingent on our world. That is to say, they receive their vital power from our world, their source which they can do no more than copy in various ways on progressively lower planes. Just as it is true for the higher worlds that it is man and only man who is able to choose and perform good, so it is only man who can do evil. Whatever man does in turn creates and gives forth an abundance of life; his whole spiritual being is involved in each act, and the angel formed thereby accompanies him as his handiwork, as a part of the existence encircling him. Like the angels of holiness, the angels of destruction are, to a degree, channels to transfer the plenty that, as it is transmuted from our world, descends the stairs of corruption, level after level, to the lowest depths of the worlds of abomination.

It follows that these worlds of evil act in conjunction with, and directly upon, man, whether in natural, concrete forms or in abstract spiritual forms. The subversive angels are thus also tempters and the inciters to evil, because they bring the knowledge of evil from their world to our world. And at the same time, the more evil a human being does, the more life-force do these angels draw from him for their world.

On the other hand, these same subversive angels also serve as an instrument for punishing the sinner. For the sinner is punished by the inevitable consequences of his deeds, just as the *zaddik* or saint receives his reward in the consequences of his benevolent deeds. In short, the sinner is punished by the closing of the circle, by being brought into contact with the domain of evil he creates. The subversive angels are revealed in a variety of forms, in both material and spiritual ways, and in their revelation they punish man for his sins in this world of ours, making him suffer torment and pain, defeat and anguish, physically as well as spiritually. The subversive angels act in one sense as manifestations and messengers of evil, and yet in another sense they constitute a necessary part of the totality of existence. For although, like the worlds of evil in general, the subversive angels are not ideal beings, they nevertheless have a role in the world, enabling it to function as it does. To be sure, were the world to root out all evil completely, then as a matter of course the subversive angels would disappear, since they exist as permanent parasites living on man. But as long as man chooses evil, he supports and nurtures whole worlds and mansions of evil, all of them drawing upon the same human sickness of soul. In fact, these worlds and mansions of evil even stir up these sicknesses and are integral to the pain and sufferings they cause. In this sense, the very origin of the demons is conditioned by the factors they influence—like a police force whose existence is useful and necessary only because of the existence of crime. The spiritual implication of the subversive angels constitutes, in addition to their negative function, a framework intended to keep the world from sliding into evil.

The fact remains, however, that these angels grow in strength and power, constantly reinforced by the growing evil in the world. Their existence is thus two-sided and ambiguous: on one hand, the main reason for their creation is to serve as a deterrent and as a limit (and in this sense they are a necessary part of the overall system of worlds); on the other hand, as the evil flourishes and spreads over the world because of the deeds of men, these destructive angels become increasingly independent existences, making up a whole realm that feeds on and fattens on evil. Whereupon the very reason for this realm is forgotten, and it appears to have become evil for its own sake, an end in itself. At which point in the paradox the vastness and magnificent scope of the purpose and meaning of man become evident. We see that man can liberate himself from the accumulating temptation of evil, by which act he compels the worlds of evil to shrink to their original mold; what is more, he is able to change these worlds completely so that they can be included in the system of the worlds of the holy, which occurs when that part of them which had become corrupt disappears completely, and that part of them which had served as a support and a deterrent assumes an entirely different character.

Nevertheless, so long as the world remains as it is, the subversive angels continue to exist within the very substance of the world of action, and even in domains above it, finding a place for themselves wherever there is any inclination toward the evil. But this happens because they themselves instigate and evoke the production of evil. They thus receive their life and power as the result of something they have aroused; and then finally, by their very existence, they constitute a punishment for the things they have helped to bring about. The worlds and the mansions of evil belong, in this sense, to the general framework of the world of action, and one of their most extreme aspects is that mansion called "Hell," in all its forms. For when the soul of man leaves the body and can relate directly to spiritual essences, thus becoming altogether spiritual, with no more than fragmented memories of having been connected with the body, then in the course of things, all that this soul had done in life casts it into its right form on the level appropriate to it in the life after death. And therefore the soul of the sinner descends, as it is symbolically expressed, to Hell. In other words, the soul now finds itself wholly within the world-domain of these subversive angels whom it, as a sinner, created; and there is no refuge from them, for these creatures encompass the soul completely and keep punishing it with full, exacting punishment for having produced them, for having caused the existence of those same angels. And as long as the just measure of anguish is not exhausted, this soul remains in Hell. Which is to say, the soul is punished not by something extraneous but by that manifestation of evil it itself created according to its level and according to its essence. Only after the soul passes through the sickness, torment, and pain of the spiritual existence of its own self-produced evil, only then can it reach a higher level of being in accordance with its correct state and in accordance with the essence of the good it created.

Since even this domain of the worlds of evil is fundamentally inward and spiritual, it is revealed only by way of vision of one kind or another. And therefore the many anthropomorphic descriptions of the subversive angels are not unlike the description of the holy angels in their crudity and their clumsy approximations. For it is not given to transmit something that does not lend itself to material description, and the imagery used is invariably inadequate.

2

Divine Manifestation

THE HOLY ONE, Blessed be He, has any number of names. All of these names, however, designate only various aspects of divine manifestation in the world, in particular as these are made known to human beings. Above and beyond this variety of designations is the divine essence itself, which has not, and cannot have, a name. We call this essence, or God-in-Himself, by a name that is itself a paradox: "the Infinite, Blessed be He."

This term, then, is meant to apply to the divine essence in itself, which cannot be called by any other name since the only name that can be applied to the very essence of God must include both the distant and the near—indeed everything. Now as we know, in the realms of abstract thought, such as mathematics and philosophy, infinity is that which is beyond measure and beyond grasp, while at the same time the term is limited by its very definition to being a quality of something finite. Thus, for example, there are many things in the world, such as numbers, that may have infinity as one of their attributes and yet also be limited either in function or purpose or in their very nature. But when we speak of the Infinite, Blessed be He, we mean the utmost of perfection and abstraction, that which encompasses everything and is beyond all possible limits.

The only thing we are permitted to say about the Infinite then, would involve the negative of all qualities. For the Infinite is beyond anything that can be grasped in *any* terms—either positive or negative. Not only is it impossible to say of the Infinite that He is in any way limited or that He is bad, one cannot even say the opposite, that He is vast or He is good. Just as He is not matter, He is not spirit, nor can He be said to exist in any dimension meaningful to us. The dilemma posed by this meaning of infinity is more than a consequence of the inadequacy of the human mind. It represents a simply unbridgeable gap, a gap that cannot be crossed by anything definable.

There would, therefore, seem to be an abyss stretching between God and the world—and not only the physical world of time, space, and gravity, but also the spiritual worlds, no matter how sublime, confined as each one is within the boundaries of its own definition. Creation itself becomes a divine paradox.

To bridge the abyss, the Infinite keeps creating the world. His creation being not the act of forming something out of nothing but the act of revelation. Creation is an emanation from the divine light; its secret is not the coming into existence of something new but the transmutation of the divine reality into something defined and limited—into a world. This transmutation involves a process, or a mystery, of contraction. God hides Himself, putting aside His essential infiniteness and withholding His endless light to the extent necessary in order that the world may exist. Within the actual divine light nothing can maintain its own existence; the world becomes possible only through the special act of divine withdrawal or contraction. Such divine non-being, or concealment, is thus the elementary condition for the existence of that which is finite.

Still, even though it appears as an entity in itself, the world is formed and sustained by the divine power manifested in this primal essence. The manifestation takes the form of ten *Sefirot*, fundamental forces or channels of divine flow. And these *Sefirot*, which are the means of divine revelation, are related to the primary divine light as a body is related to the soul; they are in the nature of an instrument or a vehicle of expression, as though a mode of creation in another dimension of existence. Or, the ten *Sefirot* can also be seen as an arrangement or configuration resembling an upright human figure, each of whose main limbs corresponds to one of the *Sefirot*. The world does not, therefore, relate directly to the hidden Godhead, which in this imagery is like the soul in relation to the human semblance of the *Sefirot*; rather, it relates to the divine manifestation, when and how this manifestation occurs, in the ten *Sefirot*. Just as a man's true soul, his inapprehensible self, is never revealed to others but manifests itself through his mind, emotions, and body, so is the Self of God not revealed in His original essence except through the ten *Sefirot*.

The ten *Sefirot* taken together constitute a fundamental and all-inclusive Reality; moreover, the pattern of this Reality is organic, each of the *Sefirot* has a unique function, complements each of the others, and is essential for the realization or fulfillment of the others and of the whole.

Because of their profound many-sidedness, the ten *Sefirot* seem to be shrouded in mystery. And there are indeed so many apparently unconnected levels of meaning to each—the levels, moreover, appearing to be unconnected—that a mere listing of their names does not adequately convey their essence. To say that the first *Sefirah*, *Keter* ("crown"), is the basic divine will and also the source of all delight and pleasure, only touches the surface. As is true with *Hokhmah* ("wisdom"), which is intuitive, instantaneous knowledge, while *Binah* ("understanding") tends more to logical analysis. *Daat* ("knowledge") is different from both, being not only the accumulation or the summation of that which is known, but a sort of eleventh *Sefirah*—belonging and yet not belonging to the ten. *Hesed* ("grace") is thus the fourth *Sefirah* and is the irrepressibly expanding impulse, or *Gedulah* ("greatness"), of love and growth. *Gevurah* ("power") is restraint and concentration, control as well as fear and awe; while *Tiferet* ("beauty") is the combination of harmony, truth, compassion. *Netzah* ("eternity") is conquest or the capacity for overcoming; *Hod* ("splendor") can also be seen as persistence or holding on; and *Yesod* ("foundation") is, among other things, the vehicle, the carrier from one thing or condition to another. *Malkhut* ("kingdom"), the tenth and last *Sefirah* is, besides sovereignty or rule, the word and the ultimate receptacle.

Keter

Binah   Hokhmah

(Daat)

Gevurah   Hesed

Tiferet

Hod   Netzah

Yesod

Malkhut

All these *Sefirot* are infinite in their potency, even though they are finite in their essence. They never appear separately, each in a pure state, but always in some sort of combination, in a variety of forms. And every single combination, or detail of such a combination, expresses a different revelation.

The great sum of all these *Sefirot* in their relatedness constitutes the permanent connection between God and His world. This connection actually operates two ways; for the world can respond and even act on its own. On the one hand, the ten *Sefirot* are responsible for the universal law and order, what we might call the workings of nature in the worlds. As such they mix and descend, contracting and changing forms as they go from one world to another, until they reach our physical world which is the final station of the manifestation of divine power.

On the other hand, the events that occur in our world continuously influence the ten *Sefirot*, affecting the nature and quality of the relations between the downpouring light and power and the recipients of this light and power.

An old allegory illustrates this influence by depicting the world as a small island in the middle of the sea, inhabited by birds. To provide them with sustenance, the king has arranged an intricate network of channels through which the necessary food and water flow. So long as the birds behave as they are endowed by nature to behave, singing and soaring through the air, the flow of plenty proceeds without interruption. But when the birds begin to play in the dirt and peck at the channels, the channels get blocked or broken and cease to function properly, and the flow from above is disrupted. So, too, does the island that is our world depend on the proper functioning of the *Sefirot*; and when they are interfered with, the system is disrupted, and the disrupting factors themselves suffer the consequences.

In this sense, the entire order of the *Sefirot*, with its laws of action and reaction, is in many ways mechanical. Nevertheless, man, who is the only creature capable of free action in the system, can cause alterations of varying degrees in the pattern and the operation. For everything man does has significance. An evil act will generally cause some disruption or negative reaction in the vast system of the *Sefirot*; and a good act, correct or raise things to a higher level. Each of the reactions extends out into all of the worlds and comes back into our own, back upon ourselves, in one form or another.

In this vast sublime order, the *mitzvot*—study and practice of the Torah, prayer, love, repentance—constitute only details or guidelines. The mitzvot teach us how certain acts, thoughts, and ways of doing things affect the *Sefirot* and bring about a desirable combination of blessedness and plenty, making the world better. In fact, before the performance of every *mitzvah* there are certain words to be said aloud—words intended to cause a great abundance to flow in from the higher worlds in order to illuminate our souls. Which means that every *mitzvah* has a specific essence through which it influences the system of the worlds and creates a certain kind of connection between the worlds and man. Thus, even though from many points of view our world is small, it can be seen as the point of intersection of all the other worlds, principally because of this power of human beings, creatures possessed of free will, to change the fixed order of things. It is as though our world were a kind of control room from which the ten *Sefirot* in their various possible combinations can be made to operate.

A transgression—that is, a disruption of the order in the system—has two results. First, it causes a kind of short circuit and skews or distorts the descent of divine plenty. Second, the shock set off by this short circuit stimulates the world of the *kelipot*, the outer shells, and causes them in turn to set off a negative charge within the particular system that belongs to the life of the transgressor.

This is what is meant by the reward and punishment that are said to follow on every action of a human being. Nor is it only a deed that so affects the system of the *Sefirot*; it is also a thought, an intention, or any of the various stirrings of the human soul. For instance, whenever a person prays—whether he prays in the prescribed manner which is oriented toward the higher worlds, or whether he engages in private prayer, uttered aloud or merely contemplated in the heart—he is able to influence the order of events. In fact, a man's spontaneous inward motions, those that have nothing to do with either his overt actions or his conscious thoughts, frequently reach up to and act on higher levels. When a man prays to be cured of sickness, for example, he is asking for grace, for a change in a vast network of systems: from the fixed system that apportions good and evil as a whole to those secondary and fluctuating systems from which descends the physical realm with its own portion of pains and miseries. He is, in other words, requesting a rearrangement within a huge complex of interlocking orders, both in the higher worlds and in the world of nature.

This pattern of divine manifestation and human relation to it may seem to be mechanical in its determinism, but it is depicted with far more personal and symbolic imagery in the scriptural sources. That is to say, in the various religious and philosophical works of the Jewish tradition, a variety of allegorical signs and figures of speech are used to signify the same thing; so that we may read of the eye of God scanning the face of the earth, the ears of God hearing all sounds, of the Holy One, Blessed be He, being pleased or angry, smiling or weeping. All these, of course, relate to the pattern of His manifestation through the ten *Sefirot* in their various configurations, analogous as the *Sefirot* are in their parts to the organs and limbs of the human body (man being made in the image of God in his body as well as in his soul). We thus have a paradigm of the essential relationships in the universe, if not of the essences themselves; and we may speak of the right hand of God as the force or power that gives, that pours out the abundance, that helps and loves; and we may speak of the left hand as the force that restrains and protects, reduces and inflicts, recognizing the harmony, or the living connection, between everything and every other in the system of the *Sefirot*.

Thus, too, when the prophets describe their sublime vision of God, His revealing Himself in the *Sefirot*, they have to present the vision in a human context in order to be true to its emotional significance for men. Their descriptions may be considered as allegorical frameworks, using man as a metaphor for the Supreme: both in the human details they employ and in the use of the idea of man as a complete entity, a microcosm. The human hand then becomes analogous to *Hesed* ("grace"), which in another configuration can be represented as water, or light; or any other variation of a symbolic metamorphosis. Therefore, too, when someone who prays or performs a *mitzvah* relates to the higher system, he may impose images upon that system, metamorphoses of the same higher force, to the point of regarding God as a humanlike figure sitting on a throne, every feature of which expresses a revelation within the *Sefirot*, in different worlds, one above the other.

Even though the order of forces is almost infinite in its immensity and complexity and seems mechanical and automatic—and even though what seems mechanical includes not only matter and the laws of nature but also the operations of laws beyond nature, of good and evil, intention and prayer, thought and feeling—this order is nevertheless transfused with the flow of divine plenty. And in this order man, though only a tiniest part of the whole, is also an effectual and meaningful actor in it.

The fact that man is only a very small detail, a dot and less than a dot as against the Infinite, is balanced by the fact that it is precisely he in his smallness who gives each of the parts its significance. Since there is an order of causes and influences, and a prime mover of all the worlds, every single person can, in his deeds, thoughts, and aspirations, reach to every one of these points of existence. Not only is man free to act on the system, each of his deeds has—in all the worlds, in terms of space and time and of the Supreme or Ultimate Reality—immeasurable significance. In contrast to all the automatic patterns of forces functioning in the cosmos, man alone moves independently within the system. He alone is important to the manifestations because he can change them, cause them to move from one level to another. Furthermore, man—dwelling as he does in two different worlds and undergoing profound inner struggles—is given the chance to rise far beyond the level of our existence and the place in which he spiritually finds himself, and to act on higher worlds without end.

Precisely because the Divine is apprehended as an infinite, not a finite, force, everything in the cosmos, whether small or large, is only a small part of the pattern, so that there is no difference in weight or gravity between any one part and another. The movement of a man's finger is as important or unimportant as the most terrible catastrophe, for as against the Infinite both are of the same dimension. Just as the Infinite can be defined as unlimited in the sense of being *beyond* everything, so He can be defined as being close to and touching everything. Here is the point of the personal human contact, for in spite of the vastness and order of all those systems, the independent acts of man—his *mitzvot* and his transgressions—cannot be explained in terms either of mechanics or, on the other hand, of magic.

When one relates only to the *Sefirot*, one is not relating to anything real. For deeds or thoughts do not operate by themselves separate from the Infinite, He who is the very life of the worlds. All the systems of the ten *Sefirot*, even though they carry out the laws of nature and beyond nature, have nothing real in themselves. In relation to the Infinite Light Himself they are less than a nothingness clothed or covered by an appearance of something real; they are only names, designations, points of departure for establishing a relationship, having nothing substantial in themselves. So that prayer, repentance, the cry of man to God, even though they are dependent upon and cut across a limited, deterministic system, neither work upon nor even address that system.

When man reaches certain heights, he learns more about God, the order and arrangement of things, relationships between one action and another, and the power and significance of law. Nevertheless, in the last resort the relationship to the Divine is individual. It is a completely private affair, the relationship of the single man in all his uniqueness of self and personality, oblivious of the infinite distance between himself and God, precisely because God in His being infinitely distant, beyond any possible contact, is Himself the One who creates the ways, the means of contact, in which every thought, every tremor of anticipation and desire on the part of man work their way until they reach the Holy One Himself, the Infinite, Blessed be He.

3

The Soul of Man

THE HUMAN SOUL, from its lowest to its highest levels, is a unique and single entity, even though it is many-faceted. In its profoundest being, the soul of man is a part of the Divine and, in this respect, is a manifestation of God in the world. To be sure, the world as a whole may be viewed as a divine manifestation, but the world remains as something else than God, while the soul of man, in its depths, may be considered to be a part of God. Indeed, only man, by virtue of his divine soul, has the potential, and some of the actual capacity, of God Himself. This potential expresses itself as the ability to go beyond the limits of a given existence, to move freely, and choose other paths, enabling man to reach the utmost heights—or to plumb the deepest hells. It is, in other words, the power to will and to create.

Man's free will thus derives its unique potential from the fact that it is a part of the divine will, without limit and without restriction. Man's creative power is also derived from the same divine power to create things that never existed before, to destroy things already in existence, and to fashion new forms. In this sense, too, man is made in the image of God.

Understandably, the Divine does not appear in man in all the infinity of being; and we speak of only an aspect of God, or of a divine spark, as constituting the essence of the inner life of man. However veiled and masked, in its broader context the human race may also be considered the manifestation of God in the world. And each and every person is an intrinsic part of this divine source of light, the point of essence. Which essential point and source is known at a certain level as the *Shekhinah*, and at another level as *Knesset Israel*, the divine vitalizing power, giving life to the world. *Knesset Israel* is the pool in which all the souls in the world are contained as a single essence, although it does not reveal itself as such, for in the world only a glimmer of the sparks of holiness in certain people is revealed. Every soul is thus a fragment of the divine light. As a spark, a part containing something of the whole, the soul's essential wholeness cannot be achieved except through effort, through work with the greater whole.

Nevertheless, in spite of all the bonds uniting the individual soul either with a higher source or with every other soul, each particular spark, each individual soul, is unique and special, in terms of its essence, its capacity, and what is demanded of it. No two souls coincide in their actions, their functions, and their paths. No one soul can take the place of another, and even the greatest of the great cannot fill the special role, the particular place, of another that may be the smallest of the small. From this notion, incidentally, derives Judaism's profound respect for human life. The life of a person is something that has no possible substitute or exchange; nothing and no one can take its place.

The soul as a primal existence—that is, prior to its connection with the world of action, or the physical world—is thus already a distinct spiritual entity in that it is a special combination of various *Sefirot* from different worlds. No soul belongs only to one *Sefirah*, even though in every soul there is a tendency to manifest more of one *Sefirah* than of others. Generally, souls are the product of combinations among *Sefirot*; and there may be hundreds and thousands of such combinations in a vast variety of forms, in a single soul. Human souls may be said to differ, then, according to the difference in the *Sefirot* making up the combination and in the combination itself, as well as in the level of the worlds out of which the soul is manifested. All of which is still in the realm of the spiritual and the abstract.

The principal action of the soul, however, its paramount importance, lies not in its abstractness, its remoteness from the physical world, but precisely in the world of living creatures, in its contact with matter. Because within the extremely complex system of relations between the soul and the world of material substance as a whole—especially relations with its own body—the soul is able to reach far higher levels than it can in its abstract state of separate essence, in what is known as the paradisiacal state outside the body. The process of the soul's connection with the body—called the "descent of the soul into matter"—is, from a certain perspective, the soul's profound tragedy. But the soul undertakes this terrible risk as a part of the need to descend in order to make the desired ascent to hitherto unknown heights. It is a risk and a danger, because the soul's connection with the body and its contact with the material world where it is the only factor that is free—unbounded by the determinism of physical law and able to choose and move freely—make it possible for the soul to fall and, in falling, to destroy the world. Indeed, Creation itself, and the creation of man, is precisely such a risk, a descent for the sake of ascension.

The soul is of course immaterial, and it is not only beyond matter but also beyond what is considered spirit: that is, it is beyond whatever the intellect, at its highest, can reach and understand or make clear to itself. The soul is thus not to be conceived as a certain defined essence, caged in the body, or even as a point or immaterial substance, but rather as a continuous line of spiritual being, stretching from the general source of all the souls to beyond the specific body of a particular person. The connection between the body and the soul is like what occurs at the end of a line of light, when a dark body is illuminated. And because the soul is not a single point in space, it should be viewed not as a single existence having one quality or character, but as many existences, on a variety of spiritual levels, one next to the other, above and beyond one another. Thus, to begin with, the soul gives the body its life and being, that vital being which distinguishes anything alive and real. Beyond this it provides the individual person with his special character and thereby fixes the way to participate in the reality of creaturely life in the world.

In other words, a human soul, at its most primary level, animates existence in terms of life force, movement, and propagation of the species; and then, on another level, it acts as the source of man's capacity to think, to imagine, to dream, to contemplate. The divine spark that is the soul thus vitalizes the human body with the essence of the life of living creatures, but in a manner far more complex and potent than in other forms of life. In spite of this added complexity of mind and emotion, this level of the soul is called the "animal soul" in the sense that it is parallel to the souls of other living creatures and functions, thinks, and is aware of itself as being concentrated in a particular vessel, the vessel of the body. At the same time, as we have seen, this soul, the primary, natural, animal soul of man, is not necessarily connected only with animal needs or with physical aspects of life, being as it is the source of those aspects or qualities peculiar to one as a person.

At a higher level, above this primal soul, there exists, in every human being, a divine soul. This is the first spark of consciousness beyond that of the zoological species, beyond even the consciousness of a higher or more developed animal, and is directly connected to divine essence. This connection of the divine soul, in the form of a line drawn from above, extends from the primal level called "Soul" which exists in one form or another in every Jew. It exists in each and every individual being, hidden and veiled as a spark of a higher perception, of a superior aspiration, and touches the higher level, which is Spirit. This level corresponds to the higher world, above our known world of action, called the "world of formation." In other words, that level of the soul of man, known as "spirit," corresponds in its inner essence to the level of an angel in the world of formation.

Beyond this there is a third level, called *Neshama* ("higher soul"), which corresponds to the level of being in the world of creation, which is still higher and more pure. Above this, above the level of *Neshama*, there is a level called *Chaya*, which corresponds to the action of the forces of the *Sefirot* in the world of emanation. And beyond all these, the most inward point of the divine spark, is the one called *Yekhida*, which may be considered the point of contact between the soul and the very essence of the Divine.

Just as the union of body and soul gives life to the body, so does it wrap the soul in material substance, providing it with the powers of the physical body. This is not a one-way process. The soul not only gives something to the body, vital force and life, it also gets something from the body, from the body's connection with matter and form, its physical capacities, its channels of perception, and its various links with both the material and the immaterial worlds. In this way, the soul is of course limited and restricted by the body; but it also draws on a new form of being, a different point of view. The contact and mutual attraction between body and soul creates a contingency, a unique situation, generating the human self, which is neither body nor soul but a merging of the two. This conjoined self can achieve great things, giving expression to the glory of the body in being raised from the inertness of matter and to the exhilaration of the soul's response to this mutual contact.

Except that the self is not a particular point, an intersection in space or a specific essence, and so differs for all men, and even for the same man himself at various stages of his development. In the first stages of life, for instance, the existence of the self is concentrated almost entirely in the life of the body, while the higher levels of mind and spirit do not show themselves except in unconscious form. With growth, with the development of the physical and spiritual powers, a person becomes increasingly aware of the higher essence of his soul, in accordance with his capacities. A person may realize his spiritual potential as a man and go beyond, if he makes the effort, to the realm of the Divine in him. But always there will remain within his life and consciousness powers drawn from his body, from the contact of his body with matter and with the various physical and spiritual beings in the world. Part of these are in the self as forms of consciousness, and part are not conscious. For the unconscious essences of being persist also in the higher aspects of the soul. The progress toward perfection, therefore, depends on one's capacity to raise the self to the level of an identification with a higher mind beyond that of contact between matter and spirit. It is an ascent of higher consciousness which proceeds from realms of the spirit to the Soul and, in extremely rare instances, to still higher levels of *Chaya*, which corresponds to the level of revelation in prophecy, when the self receives power and plenitude directly and consciously from the world of emanation.

Thus consciousness, assuming ever new identification along the lifeline of the soul, is the way of man's ascent to perfection. The more one rises, the closer one comes to the realization of the highest purpose of one's being. To be sure, only very few people are ever privileged to reach these highest levels; and even when they do reach them, it is not to remain, but to experience an occasional flash of awareness of the higher existence within. Only the greatest of men achieve this level where the self exists, in terms of consciousness, in the world of emanation. The rest of mankind lives on the level of the world of action or scarcely above it. They can rise a little—if, indeed, they manage to do so at all—only by virtue of their choice, their deeds, their sincerest efforts.

Since the soul is of the inner essence of the *Sefirot*, it must necessarily manifest the structures of the ten *Sefirot* in real life; for the ten *Sefirot* are the instruments of the Supreme Omnipotence. Thus, when man lives in a state of perfection, without any distortion of his being, his soul and the relations between his soul and his body reflect the whole world and the ten supreme *Sefirot*, and he can say: "Yet in my flesh shall I see God" (Job 19:26). Man in his purity should be able to perceive the whole order of relations between God and the world, and the order of relations within the *Sefirot* as this is reflected in the microcosm of his human existence. Just as they do in the higher world, the ten *Sefirot* exist in the human soul; and from their mutual interrelations are derived and manifested all the broad span of thoughts, feelings, and experiences of man. Thus, the first three *Sefirot* assert the aspects of pure consciousness: *Hokhmah*, expressing the power of original light, is that which distinguishes and creates and is the basis of intuitive grasp; *Binah*, expressing the analytical and synthetic power of the mind, builds and comprehends forms and probes the meaning of that which comes from the *Sefirah* of *Hokhmah*; and *Daat*, expressing the crystallization of awareness in terms of conclusions and the abstract ascertaining of facts, is that which enables consciousness to make a transition from one form of existence to another, thereby ensuring its continuity. Then following these are the three *Sefirot* of the higher emotions: *Hesed*, *Gevurah*, and *Tiferet*. *Hesed* as grace and love is the inclination toward things, the desire for, or attraction to beings, the outgoing flow and opening up to the world, that which gives of itself, whether in terms of will or affection or relation and, in giving, opens up to the *Sefirah* of *Gevurah*, or strength. *Gevurah* is thus an inward withdrawal of forces, a concentration of power which provides an energy source for hate, fear, and terror as well as for justice, restraint, and control. *Tiferet* is harmony and compassion as well as beauty, being a synthesis or a balancing of the higher powers of attraction and repulsion, and leads to moral as well as to aesthetic acceptance of the world. From these we proceed to the three *Sefirot* that act directly on the actual world of experience: *Netzah*, *Hod*, and *Yesod.* Netzah is the will to overcome, the profound urge to get things done. *Hod*, in striving to achieve and attain that which is desired, is also the power to repudiate the obstacles that rise from reality, and to persevere. *Yesod* is the power of connection, the capacity and the will to build bridges, make contacts, and relate to others, especially in the way this is done with teacher, father, and other figures of meaning and authority. Finally, the *Sefirah* of *Malkhut* is the realization, or living through, of this potential in the essential being: it is the transition from soul to outer existence, to thought, and to deed. It also effects the transmutation of consciousness back to *Keter*, the first and highest of the *Sefirot*, which is also the essence of will and contains in itself all the higher powers that activate the soul from above.

These basic powers combine and work together; two or more of them bring about an event or activate something and together create the thoughts and feelings of man in all their enormous subtlety and complexity. Thus every single thought, emotion, or action is a result of the combination of forces of one or another or all of the *Sefirot*, every compounding of which expresses a particular essence, being, or creation in the world.

The soul of man functions through its instrument or vessel, which is the body. Through it and with it, the soul thinks, perceives, feels, and acts; through it and by it, the soul has to fulfill its double function in reality. First, it has to perform a certain task in the process of perfecting the outer world, or at least that part of the world to which it is destined. And second, its task is to raise itself. But these tasks are not necessarily separate; they are accomplished simultaneously. For the physical world contains in itself a higher essence, higher forces, in which, even though hidden and distorted, there exist elements of the original divine formlessness. It is with these higher forces that the soul, in its work of *Tikkun*, or correction, is united; and in thus raising a portion of the world, it is also raised and uplifted. The relation between body and soul, and altogether between the spirit of things and their corporeality, may be expressed by the example of a rider on horseback. A rider who is in control and guides his steed can go much farther than he can go on foot. How aptly then does the image of the Messiah as a poor man riding on a donkey describe the human predicament; the divine spark borne and guiding, the physical donkey bearing up and waiting for guidance and power.

Zach 9.9

The path of *Tikkun*, the course plotted for the soul's sojourn in the world, is generally found in the Torah, which is supposed to be a guiding instrument. For the Torah is not only a higher revelation; it is a practical guide to direct man on the way, showing him what to do and how to do it in his task of repairing the world. Within this general course or task of raising the level of the universe, each and every soul has to find its own particular way, its own place, and the specific objects relating to its existence. Therefore, it has been said that each of the letters of the Torah has some corresponding soul; that is to say, every soul is a letter in the entire Torah, and has its own part to play. The soul that has fulfilled its task, that has done what it has to do in terms of creating or repairing its own part of the world and realizing its own essence, can wait after death for the perfection of the world as a whole. But not all the souls are so privileged: many stray for one reason or another; sometimes a person does not do all the proper things, and sometimes he misuses forces and spoils his portion and the portion of others. In such cases the soul does not complete its task and may even itself be damaged by contact with the world. It has not managed to complete that portion of reality which only this particular soul can complete; and therefore, after the death of the body, the soul returns and is reincarnated in the body of another person and again must try and complete what it failed to correct or what it injured in the past. The sins of man are not eliminated so long as this soul does not complete that which it has to complete. From which it may be seen that most souls are not new, they are not in the world for the first time. Almost every person bears the legacy of previous existences. Generally one does not obtain the previous self again, for the soul manifests itself in different circumstances and in different situations. What is more, some souls are compounded of more than one single former person and share parts of a number of persons. A great soul is most usually reincarnated not in one single body but branches out, participating in a number of people, each of whom have to satisfy different aspects of existence. In spite of this incalculable complexity, the soul will be made up of the same constituent elements and will have to complete those uncompleted tasks left over from the previous cycle. Therefore the destiny of a person is connected not only with those things he himself creates and does, but also with what happens to the soul in its previous incarnations. The encounters and events of life, its joys and sorrows, are influenced by one's previous existence. One's existence is a continuity, the sustaining of a certain fundamental essence; and certain elements may rise to the surface which do not seem to belong to the present, which a person has to complete or fix or correct—a portion of the world it is his task to put right in order for him to raise his soul to its proper level.

And this struggle of the souls is also the struggle and way of the world toward its redemption. As the souls return and strive to correct the world and vindicate themselves, at a certain level of this overall *Tikkun* or correction they reach their highest peak. Then the greatest obstacles are behind the human race, and it can go forward toward its perfection with sure steps and without the legacy of suffering inherited from previous existences and previous sins—this is the beginning of Salvation, which is the time of the Messiah. In this manner man proceeds until that stage is reached when all the souls return, each to its own self, when every self in the world will enter into a new life in complete fusion with the higher forces of the soul on all levels and of the body, manifesting all the potential powers it contains. This level of the perfection of all humanity, in which a new relation will exist between body and soul, and the world will be whole with itself, is called "Heaven" or the "next world." It is the goal toward which all the souls of men, in discharging their private and specific tasks in life, aspire and strive.

4

Holiness

THE ROOT MEANING of the concept of "the holy" in the holy language is separation: it implies the apartness and remoteness of something. The holy is that which is out of bounds, untouchable, and altogether beyond grasp; it cannot be understood or even defined, being so totally unlike anything else. To be holy is, in essence, to be distinctly other.

There is much in the world that may be great, good, noble, or beautiful without necessarily comprising any part of the essence of the holy, for the holy is beyond qualification. In fact, it cannot be described in any way other than by the very highest of all designations—that is, as "holy." The designation itself is the repudiation of all other names and titles.

Consequently, the only one who can be called holy is God; and the Holy One, Blessed be He, the Highest and the Holy One, is unlike all else, being immeasurably remote, elevated, and transcendent. Nevertheless, we do speak of the dissemination of holiness over the world, over all the worlds, according to their levels and even over this world of ours, in all its constituent parts—time, place, and soul. And, in fact, we are even able to increase our receptivity to holiness by opening ourselves to its influence.

The holiness of place is manifested in a series of concentric circles, at the center of which is the Holy of Holies in Jerusalem. In itself, the Holy Temple is only a sort of "spiritual implement," built precisely according to the instructions of the Torah and the words of the prophets for the purpose of helping to anchor holiness in the material world—that is to say, to serve as a focal point of contact between the unreachable Supreme Holiness and the actuality of place. The overall design of the Temple, in all its details from the outer courts to ritual objects and vessels, is a kind of projection of the higher world onto our world. Each part of the Temple can, from a certain point of view, be seen as homogeneous with a whole order of worlds beyond us. Or, to put it another way, the Temple in all its detail is a symbolic model of the Chariot; and the Holy of Holies is the place of the revelation of the divine glory, the point of contact, or of intersection, among the different worlds and between one level of existence and another.

The Holy of Holies is therefore a point situated in our world and other worlds at the same time. As such it is a place subject to the laws of all the worlds, and so outside the ordinary laws of time and place. That is why the Holy of Holies was barred to all men, except for the brief entry of the high priest of Israel once a year, on the Day of Atonement.

As may be surmised, the holiness of this place is made manifest only when everything is as it should be, when the Temple stands at its appointed location, and when everything in the Temple is so perfectly ordered and arranged that it is pervaded by the *Shekhinah*. Since, however, the site chosen (by prophetic revelation) is that one place in space where such a divine connection can be made at all times, the holiness of the site persists even when the Temple itself is no longer there. So that even though this holiness may not be manifest now, the possibility of its manifestation is eternal. From the Temple site the circles of holiness extend ever farther into space, becoming fainter as they recede from the Holy of Holies to the Temple Court, from the Temple Court to the Holy City of Jerusalem, from the Holy City of Jerusalem to all of the Holy Land, and then, of course, beyond. Each of these bounded spaces implies a wide range of obligations and privileges. The holier a place is, the more strict is the general obligation—in addition to all the more specific obligations devolving upon those who live or, like priests, function in a sanctified area—to relate to it in a certain way.

Though the potential for holiness persists forever, it is true that the holiness of the Land of Israel cannot be adequately manifested unless all the constituents of the circles of sanctity radiating from the center in Jerusalem are in their proper places. Thus, when the Temple is not standing, all the aspects of holiness that grow out of it become vague and uncertain, some of them sinking into a state of only latent sanctity, indicating no more than a possibility and a starting point. The holiness of the Holy Land has nothing to do with who the inhabitants are or what they do; it is a choice from on high, beyond human comprehension.

The sanctity of place is objective, a thing in its own right. But in order to be conscious of this sanctity, one has to be vouchsafed a certain experience. For it is seldom that holiness is *space*

made externally evident in the material world. The sites where it is recognized are often used for the deepest efforts to invoke the Supreme Source of plenty. Nor does the revelation of holiness at some particular place always have a totally positive effect; for in order to be properly receptive to holiness, one needs to have attained a high degree of purification. In the absence of consciousness and purification, the sense of holiness may be obscured or even scarcely grasped at all, and consequently, its effect may be the very opposite of sanctification. Indeed, the powerful uplifting appeal of a holy place is frequently counterbalanced by feelings precisely of denial and rebellion against its holiness. Because wherever there is holiness, there are also those parasitic forces irresistibly attracted to holiness, seeking to live off it and at the same time to destroy it. Only when the entire apparatus of revelation is fixed and arranged to perfection can a holy site reveal itself to every man, without distinction, irrespective of people's subjective states of mind or of the presence of parasitic destructive forces.

The holiness of a place would therefore imply that there had been some revelation of the Supreme Holiness at a point in physical space chosen to be a vehicle of the divine plenty. There are other kinds of sacred places, to be sure—places that have not attained holiness in this complete sense of the term but have nevertheless come under the influence of some holy occurrence or personality. The tombs of saints and sages, for instance, or the places where they performed memorable deeds may acquire great spiritual value. But such sites are not of the same order as, and are not to be confused with, that true connection between God and place which has been revealed in the radiating sanctity of the Holy Temple.

Holiness is manifested also in time, and there are consecrated days in the week, the month, and the year. The concept of time in the Jewish way of thinking is not one of a linear flow. Time is a process, in which past, present, and future are bound to each other, not only by cause and effect but also as a harmonization of two motions: progress forward and a countermotion backward, encircling and returning. It is more like a spiral, or a helix, rising up from Creation. There is always a certain return to the past; and the past is never a condition that has gone by and is no more, but rather one that continually returns and begins again at some significant point whose significance changes constantly according to changing circumstances. There is thus a constant reversion to basic patterns of the past, although it is never possible to have a precise counterpart of any moment of time.

The scope of this return to the past is diverse, the movement ranging through a number of circles, intersecting and interlocking with one another. The primary circuit is that of day and night; thereafter there are the week, the month, and the year, the half-century cycles of the jubilee, and the great cycles of a thousand years and of seven thousand years.

The round of the week is a kind of recapitulation of the seven days of Creation. Each day of the week is not only an occasion to mark the particular work of creation of that day but also a framework within which is manifested the special quality of existence corresponding to one of the *Sefirot*. For, as it would appear, the seven days of the week, and the particular thing created on each of the days as told us in Genesis, are emanations of the higher *Sefirot* into time. Thus there are days of the week that belong to certain kinds of action or states of mind, and others fit for other modes of being. Tuesday, for example, being the manifestation of the *Sefirah* of *Tiferet* ("beauty" or "harmony") is considered a day given to success and good fortune. While Monday, the day of the *Sefirah* of *Gevurah,* and Wednesday are considered to have a sometimes hurtful severity.

Also, the hours and portions of the day have their rhythmic patterns according to the subtle influences of the *Sefirot* as reflected by the slanting rays of the sun. The morning hours are the well-favored ones; the afternoon is largely under the influence of the *Sefirah of Gevurah,* growing ever more stern as evening approaches; while the time from midnight to dawn is the time for the manifestation of the finer and gentler qualities of *Tiferet.*

The Sabbath is not just another day of the week, nor even a special day; it sums up the week and gives meaning to it. The weekdays are marked by the acts of Creation, ever repeated by the descent of the divine plenty into the world. And parallel to this descent it is man's function during the week, in the order of things, to fix and to set the world right wherever it tends to go wrong. This includes correcting the world, in the physical sense, by work and action on the external frame and, in the spiritual sense, perfecting the world by performing *mitzvot.* For in the realm of the human soul, man's work on himself, his constant correcting of faults and spurring to activity of his inner being, constitutes a ceaseless creative effort.

The Sabbath is essentially the day of rest, of cessation from all labor and creative effort. And this holds true for the spiritual effort of working on oneself as well as for the physical effort of working on the world. The week is characterized by busyness or activity, while the Sabbath is grounded on stillness, on the nullification of oneself in the downpour of holiness. And this self-repudiation is expressed by a renunciation of all work, whether it be in the physical sense, as being busy in the world, or in the spiritual sense, as engaging in efforts to correct one's soul. In fact, the very power to receive the spiritual essence of the Sabbath comes from one's readiness and ability to surrender, to give up one's human and worldly state for the sake of the Supreme Holiness, through which all the worlds are raised to a higher level.

The round of weekdays and Sabbaths is without end. On the one hand, the weekdays prepare the Sabbath, correcting and providing additional plenty to the world, making it possible to bring things to a conclusion and to raise them to a suitably higher level. On the other hand, the Sabbath is the source of plenty for all the days of the week that follow it. The surrender of oneself on the Sabbath is not simply a matter of no activity but of opening oneself to the influence of the higher worlds and thereby receiving the strength for all the days of the week that follow.

Like the sanctity of a place, the sanctity of a day, of a certain unit of time, is intrinsic to it and cannot be transferred to another day. Nevertheless, the experience of this holiness, objective as it is, depends on one's spiritual readiness and openness. The more intensive and sincere the preparations during the week in the secular course of a person's life, the more holy is the Sabbath. The higher the spiritual level of a person in general, the more keenly is the sense of the general uplift—a raising of all the worlds—felt on this day. Thus, although the round of the weekdays and the Sabbath is endlessly repeated, it is never the same. There are subtle variations in the flow of plenty, just as men themselves differ. And still, every single week is an archetype, a recapitulation of the primordial pattern of Genesis.

The cycles of the month and the year are somewhat different, bound as they are to natural events, like the motions of the sun and the moon, or to social-national events that have assumed a meaning beyond the historical. The Jewish month, for instance, is a lunar cycle, related solely to the phases of the moon: the waxing moon constitutes the beginning of the month, and the waning moon its latter part; and most of the holidays come at the time of the full moon or near it. Simultaneously, the first of the month, at the time of the new moon, has a special position in the round of the year. The annual cycle of the sun, however, relies for its sanctity on the festivals and holy days, when a revelatory event in the historic past and the divinely determined future are ritually bound to the present.

It is in this way that holy days are connected to significant historic happenings, such as the Exodus from Egypt on Passover, the receiving of the Torah on Mount Sinai on *Shavuot* (Pentecost), or the wanderings of the Children of Israel in the wilderness on *Succot* (Tabernacles). These holy festivals are not intended simply as memorial days to keep alive the memory of the events; they are divinely appointed times dedicated to a renewal of the same revelation that once occurred on that day in the year, a repetition and a restoration of the same forces. So that the sanctity of the holidays is derived not only from a primal divine revelation but also from Israel's continual resanctification, in the way it keeps these days holy, of this revelation.

Besides the holidays that recapitulate some primal revelation in history, there are holy days that serve the need to sanctify time, or the year, itself. Thus New Year's Day is, in a manner of speaking, man's first day in the created world. In the same way, Yom Kippur, the Day of Atonement, is the day when the Supreme Holiness is revealed, and man rises above all the worlds. This is made possible by the divine forgiveness and pardoning of sins, which overcome the downward pull of forces resulting from transgressions and shameful thoughts, and bring about an immense new purification of man's connection with God.

Since the sanctity of a holiday is derived not from the historic event it commemorates but from the revelation behind that event, some historic events do not deserve to be perpetuated as holy days at all. A historic event may therefore be commemorated as a memorial day only, either sad or joyous as the case may be, but not part of the order of eternally sanctified days. Thus the anniversaries of certain profoundly tragic events, like the destruction of the Temple, are counted as days of mourning throughout the generations. Only when the world attains to a certain degree of redemption can these days be allowed to fade into oblivion. Until then, certain days of the year, like the first part of the month Av, are considered days of mourning and misfortune, and in them calamities tend to appear, or reappear, so multiplying the force of grievous memories.

In addition to the festivals and the fasts that belong to the
nation as a whole, other days mark significant events in the ca-
reers of outstanding personalities who have had some influence
on either all of the people or a part of it, and there are days
commemorating events in the history of certain families or in
individual lives. The anniversaries of the deaths of great men
(and in Judaism only holy men are great), for instance, are considered occasions not, for the most part, for grief at the passing
of a leader, but for gaiety at remembering the sanctity of the
man and his ultimate spiritual victory in death. Also, birthdays
or other days of personal importance are frequently made part
of the individual cycle of the year. The important fact is that
the only truly holy days are those deriving their sanctity from
God—that is to say, when, at a certain date in the course of
time, the divine abundance is revealed and returns to reveal itself each and every year.

A third aspect of holiness is that of the human soul, the sanctity of man. And even this holiness does not derive from man
himself. A person may be great, wise, and full of the most excel-
lent of virtues; he may even be a *zaddik* and a Hassid; but the
essence of holiness comes to him only insofar as he is connected
to God, the source of the holy. A person may be connected
with the source of holiness in several ways. There is a holiness
that is inherited, that belongs to the family, given by God to
those who serve Him in a certain way. Here one may include
the holiness of Israel as a whole, or that of the sons of Aaron,
the hereditary priesthood. Then there is the more meaningful
consecration that comes from the communion of man with
God—such as may be attained, for example, through the

mitzvot. Adhering completely to the holy precepts for conduct and refraining entirely from wrongdoing envelops a man in a constant, ceaseless communion with God. Beyond this is the more intellectual union with the divine holiness, through study and knowledge of the Torah. When man puts his very life and soul into studying the Torah, and makes himself thoroughly familiar with the laws and the commandments, he becomes bound up in Torah, which is one of the manifestations of the Supreme Holiness. Higher still is a man's ability to surrender himself, to relinquish his own will and being to God's will. When a man reaches such a level of renunciation, he also attains a level of sanctification that reveals itself in different ways, according to his spiritual capacities.

Sometimes man surrenders himself to the divine holiness only within the realm of Torah and *mitzvot*. And striving further, he may reach a certain identification with something that is known only in terms of the higher wisdom in him. If he should attain to a union of such great force, he is able to respond to the divine influence and be vouchsafed a revelation of the Holy Spirit, and his whole life would change accordingly. This level has indeed been achieved by many great men throughout history, through an adherence to *mitzvot* and Torah and by their whole way of life. And above this level are a select few who from time to time in human history are privileged to be so receptive to the divine plenty they are given prophetic power. And even with respect to prophetic power one may distinguish levels. There are prophets to whom prophecy comes as a transient vision: they feel as though a higher power compels them and produces in them images and ideas. On a higher level is the *Shekhinah* "who speaks in the throat," when all his life the prophet is in some connection with the divine will and he himself serves as an instrument of revelation. And at the highest level of holiness are those persons who have achieved a state in which their whole personalities and all of their actions are inseparably joined to the divine holiness. Of these persons it is said that they have become a "chariot" for the *Shekhinah*, and like the Chariot, they are totally yielded up to the One who sits on the driver's seat, the throne of glory, and they constitute a part of the throne of glory itself, even though they are flesh and blood, men like all other men.

The life of a holy person becomes an example and a model for all men to follow. And a holy person may be a great king or a saintly *zaddik*, a sage or a leader of his age. But he may also be one of the hidden saints whose holiness goes unrecognized by men. But in whatever manner the holiness shows itself, and no matter how intrinsic it may be to the personality of the man, it is still dependent on his connection with the divine plenty.

The ordinary man who has been granted contact with the holy person is thereby brought into a certain contact with true holiness. In this sense, the higher the level of a saintly person's holiness, the more is he like an angel (and in a way even more than an angel), acting as a vehicle of holiness by transmitting divine plenty from one world to another and bestowing such plenty upon whomever he chooses, through his blessings, his actions, his prayers. The individual who makes inner contact with such a holy person, showing him love and devotion, thereby supports the flow of divine plenty in the world. This is what has been meant in Jewish tradition, from time immemorial, when devotion has been shown to those persons who are superior in holiness or have an aura of sanctity. The gift is given such blessed men to create a bond of some sort that will draw them nearer, whether the holy person is connected to God by being a great scholar of the Torah or whether he is just a saintly individual in his life. To honor, revere, and love the holy person is a *mitzvah* in itself, besides serving as a means for direct contact with holiness. And just as inner connection with the holiness of place or time consecrates and raises one, so does the holy person—although, to be sure, the additional factor of conscious transfer of blessedness makes this contact the most heart-stirring and consequential of all human relationships.

5

Torah

THE SCRIPTURES, beginning with the Bible and including the many works of exegesis and commentary—such as the Talmud, the Kabbalah, and other writings—occupy such a central and special place in Judaism that the Hebrew name for this sacred literature, Torah, cannot be adequately translated into any other language. As someone once aptly summed it up: other religions have a concept of scripture as deriving from Heaven, but only Judaism seems to be based on the idea that the Torah Scripture is itself Heaven. In other words, the Torah of the Jews is the essence of divine revelation; it is not only a basis for social, political, and religious life but is in itself something of supreme value.

This perception of the nature of Torah is derived from the fact that the Torah in all its different forms is a collection of concentrated emanations and transmutations of divine wisdom. Thus, the Torah as apprehended by us is only a particular aspect of that divine essence, just as the world is a particular mode of divine revelation. The Torah is, if anything, an even clearer and more perfect manifestation than the world. As the sages have said: before Creation, God looked into the Torah and made the world accordingly. By which it is implied that the Torah is the original pattern, or inner plan, of the world: Torah and world are, inseparably, a pair.

Since the Torah expresses the inner will, the direction and mode of operation of the relations between the world and God, it is the spiritual map of the universe. It is not, however, a static chart of things as they are but a dynamic plan of the ever-changing world, charting the necessary course for moving toward a union with God. This means that in its primary essence Torah is the manifestation of the divine wisdom; but like the created world, it has to be expressed through limited forms, like words, and even the physical substance that carries the words, in order to bring the revelation down to the world of action.

Intellectual and emotional immersion in Torah is therefore a way of making contact with the essence of all the worlds on various levels. For the Torah expresses the divine will, and wisdom itself, in all the worlds; whereas in the world of action the divine will express itself only in terms of the immediately surrounding reality. And the limitations of this reality in our world, which are experienced through the reign of nature, are extreme; they can be overcome only through man's freedom of choice. The relation between Torah and the world is thus the relation between idea and actualization, between vision and fulfillment. So that the intellectual study of Torah and the emotional involvement in its contents are a form of identification with the divine will, with what may be called God's dream of the existence of the world and the existence of man. One who is immersed in Torah becomes a partner of God, in the sense that man on one hand and God on the other are participating in the planning, the spinning out of the idea, the common dream of the existence of the world.

One of the means of contact between Torah and the world, then, is this emotional and intellectual contact involved in its study. But there is also another side to the Torah, that of being the Law, of compelling men to behave in certain ways. For the Torah is, to a large extent, a plan of human action and relationship, providing guidance for what is the proper way to behave, think, dream, and desire in order that the Torah's design for the world be realized. In this respect the Torah is a way of life, showing both how to relate inwardly and how to conduct oneself outwardly, practically. And that perhaps is why the word "Torah" is of the same root as the word *hora'ah* ("instruction" or "teaching"), providing as it does a guide to the path of God.

Theoretically, the perfect man can reach this identification with Torah from within himself. When a man purifies himself of all the illusions and distortions of his self-centered desires, when he opens up to the divine plenty, he can be like an instrument in the hands of the Supreme Will; and so the way he does anything will be Torah. Except that this way of reaching Torah, which derives from the power to achieve human perfection, is extremely rare, requiring a magnitude of contact with the Divine far beyond the level possible for ordinary man. Only the rarest individuals—like the patriarchs Abraham, Isaac, and Jacob—can be said to have achieved it; and even they reached the level of Torah as a way of life only with respect to their own lives and each on his own level. So it must appear to us that God's gift to the world in the divine revelation of Torah is a gift in which He bestows not only a guide to the proper life of man and not only a plan for the very existence of the world, but also Himself. Or, to put it another way, He gives what we might call His dream of the superior man who could participate with Him on all levels, whether on the level of actual human life or on the level of worlds only vaguely perceived or altogether beyond the senses.

There are many aspects to the Torah, and one can connect oneself with it in a variety of ways—in terms of abstract speculation and rational logic, of emotional involvement and, of course, of conduct. Most of the law of the Torah, however, deals with fairly practical matters: what to do and what not to do in the realm of action. Indeed, the extent to which the Torah, which has so great a significance beyond the physical world, is involved with material reality might seem surprising. It can, however, be explained in a number of ways, from above and from within. On one level, the Torah, after all, relates to people living in this world and has to deal with the reality of their lives, with all the immediacy of their need. A Torah that deals only, or mainly, with matters of higher spirituality would be cut off from contact with human existence, with its dependence on the physical world. The act of tying in with God's will by means of physical action provides a simpler, more natural, and of course, more essentially direct contact for man as he is. From within its own terms, moreover, the Torah is not really suited to an abstract contemplation of higher worlds, explicit as it is about a whole variety of relations in the human world. The behavior of a man as a particular physical action or, obversely, as the renunciation of a particular action has a significance far beyond his subjective present existence—indeed, beyond his own life. This is true not only for the many commandments that are concerned with relations between and among people, but also for those commandments that a man is to do by himself. When one is engaged with objects in the physical world, one sets off a chain of relations involving all the things and people who have in one way or another taken part in this action through time as well as in space. In this respect physical action is more profound than mental or even spiritual action, in that it is implicated in *Tikkun*, the correcting of the world, a process involved not only with the world's spiritual aspects but with the actual physical realm—that is to say, the restoration by sacred action of things to their ideal place in the world. A holy action that is entirely spiritual works only indirectly on the physical structure of the world, while a physical action works on it directly—although, to be sure, the physical substructure of the world is a part of world as a whole and not a separate realm, and all its levels of development are a part of the general system of *Tikkun* and evolution of the worlds, of their purification and preparation for God.

Another, more inward aspect is connected with the view that the material world is not inferior, that matter in itself is not lower or worse, and that in a sense the physical world may even be considered the height of Creation. It is the marvel of Creation for the paradoxical reason that the very existence of matter is a condition that seems to obscure the Divine, and thus could only be the result of a special intention on the part of the Infinite. Matter is a sort of standing wave between the manifestation of God and the hiddenness of God; it is defined by its limitations. To retain its separate and independent existence, infinite force has to be exerted on every particle. Hence, every human action that disposes matter in the direction of holiness has a qualitative significance far beyond anything like it in the world of spirituality. What is more, since the world of matter constitutes the focal point of all the other worlds, every movement, every slightest budge of things in the rigid realm of matter has an effect beyond any similar motion in the realm of the spirit and even in realms above the spirit. And thus the *mitzvah*, the law of the Torah which deals so much with matter—with the effort to exert influence on the physical world, to change it, to divert it toward holiness, even though matter itself seems to be so limited and restricted—is intended to release vast forces in all the worlds and to create waves of movement rising from our world to higher worlds without end. Which is why it may be said that a genuine holy action of any kind performed in the domain of matter, the raw material of substance, has far greater possible meaning than anything performed only in an intermediate domain of thought or emotion. For the Torah and the *mitzvot* concerned with the physical world relate to this world as though it were the secret of Creation, the essence of the fulfillment of the divine idea.

Besides its concern with the physical world, the Torah has another, perhaps disconcerting characteristic: that it does not restrict itself to one area of life, such as religion or ethics, but spreads out and covers almost all areas of existence. By definition, the way of the Torah is not religious in the strict sense of addressing only that part of a person's life concerned only with relations between the human and the Divine. The Torah is not a narrow domain of holiness a man may enter or leave as he chooses while the domain of ordinary existence remains neutral territory, where God does not interfere much, and where in any case there is not much point in trying to relate to Him. Since the Torah is the blueprint of the world, it regulates the whole and cannot be confined to any particular part. True, its directives are not all on the same level of practicality; nevertheless, its instructions and guidelines and modes of relating are valid for all situations in life. The more one becomes identified with the Torah, the more does its significance expand beyond particular circumstance. Rather than constituting itself an ideal for the monastic life, say, or a guide or for any other sort of separation from the reality of the world, Torah works in precisely the opposite fashion, introducing more content and meaning into the trivial details of the life of the world. One finds the Torah significant in every aspect of community, commerce, agriculture, and industry, in the life of feeling and love, in relations between the sexes—down to the most minute aspects of living, like buttoning one's shoes or lying down to sleep. What is surprising is that with the great quantity and range of its laws, what to do and what not to do, Torah still does not really limit the activities of an individual in any field of endeavor. That is to say, there is no field of action or thought which, in principle, the Torah repudiates. The Law, in general and in detail, theoretically and practically, mostly adds detail to action, qualifies modes of behavior, imposes new modes, directs the conduct of one's daily business from waking to sleeping—the supposition being that if all these actions are properly defined and prepared, then the guidance of the Law need not and does not change their essence, but adds a quality to them.

A pragmatic examination of the way of life that results from obedience to the Torah shows that in the long run, besides offering considerable freedom in almost every area of endeavor, such obedience lends to every act the quality of ritual and makes it seem a direct link between man and his Maker. This is true irrespective of the nature of the action, whether it be ceremonial or spontaneous, related to God or to people, internal or external. For the process of an ever deeper identification with Torah seems to have the effect of intensifying the manner in which one carries out instructions otherwise quite vague and general, even to the point that the way one walks or stands, the gestures of one's hands or face, the tones of one's speech, and so on are visibly modified. A unified pattern of life, in which act is integrated with thought and speech, music—so to speak—integrated with the maker of music, is thus eventually created. The result is something like a dance drama of cosmic dimensions in which man moves on all levels of existence, in an unbroken stylization of action. It is not to be wondered at, therefore, that external forms of artistic expression were, if not absolutely prohibited, at least severely restricted: mere aesthetic forms can only be partial and inadequate as compared with the great artistic creation of the whole way of life of a Jew living according to the Torah.

This dance of life in Judaism is so intrinsic to individual growth that, from one point of view, it may be considered a solo performance. From another point of view, the life and actions of the individual Jew form a segment of the greater entity of the nation or the people as a whole. The sacramental character of this entity is manifested by the transmission of something from one individual Jew to another, no matter how scattered the people may be. This intangible essence enters into all the deeds of the Jew and integrates with that of other individuals, making up the dance pattern for the movements of the soul of the world in its development and approach to the Divine. It is thus that the sacramental body of *Knesset Israel* (the "assembly of Israel"), the whole of the Jewish people, is conceived to be at its root the same as the *Shekhinah*. In other words, *Knesset Israel* is identical with the inner content, the essential holiness, of the world as a whole.

The Jewish definition of the election of Israel as a nation of priests and a holy people makes the Jews a people whose way of life constitutes the priesthood of the world, one whose intricate stylization of life from the most personal act of the individual to the compounded actions of its communities, its great centers of Jewish learning, its land, its Holy Temple, all constitute aspects of this function.

I do not mean to imply that holiness is in any way restricted to one people or that the approach to the Divine is not equally available to all of mankind. It is only that the Jews undertake a greater burden; with the acceptance of the Torah as an inner way of life, as an inner map, they encumber themselves with the responsibility and obligation of a priesthood not confined to a particular time or place but for all of life. From this perspective, the whole world is a holy temple, and one that has to be constantly purified and sanctified anew. The priests who come together in the precincts of this holiness constitute the heartbeat of the world, the rhythm of mankind's breathing. The obligation is therefore greater and the responsibility heavier precisely because of the feeling that this nation of priests, in its decline and disintegration, in the fall of its individuals, is not only destroying itself but in some unseen way, is impairing the way of the world as a whole, and that in its restoration and growth it leads the world to its heart and its spiritual source, the *Shekhinah*. And when the people functions as one wave, as one beat, then this habitual stylization perfects the pattern of the world, and the choreographic design of the Torah can be realized in living actuality.

6

The Way of Choice: An Answer to Ethics

Just as there is content to a man's actions and thoughts in the course of his living his life and worshiping his God, so are there proper ways for him to do things. These ways will naturally tend to express certain content of their own, reflecting his particular orientation to the inner life.

In Judaism this way is not simple, nor is it one consistent thing. Not only are there in principle many possible alternatives, but even where there are no alternatives, there is fluidity. From a certain point of view, the right style of life for the soul of man must be full of contradiction, problems, disunity, because man himself is not a single, consistent entity, either as a human being in general or as a particular individual. Every person has his own spiritual essence whose uniqueness not only is the result of his heredity and education but exists by divine intention. For each and every human being has a specific task to perform in the world, a task that no one else can accomplish, though there may well be better and more gifted people around to do it. Only he can do it in a certain way, in the singular composite of manner, personality, and circumstance that belongs to him.

Divine service in the world is divided up, with each human being, like the primordial Adam, put in charge of a certain portion of God's garden, to work it and keep it. It is said that in the Torah there are seventy faces which are the seventy faces of the divine *Shekhinah*, and that these contain six hundred thousand faces in accordance with the number of primary souls of Israel, so that every individual soul has a certain part in the Torah. In other words, each soul understands and does things in a way not suitable for another soul. Everyone can and should learn from others the proper way of doing things, but in the end each person has to follow his own winding path to the goal that is his heart's desire. Some lives have an emotional emphasis; others, an intellectual; for some the way of joy is natural; for others existence is full of effort and struggle; there are people for whom purity of heart is the most difficult thing in the world, while for others it is given as a gift from birth. What is more, not only is there no equality among people, there is even no consistency within the life of a single person. There are the great differences between the various ages of youth and maturity, and the small differences within the year, the week, the day itself, such as the Sabbath and the times of prayer. And, of course, there is the difference in the manner in which the same person will approach varying situations. Which is not meant to imply that there is no difference at all between a good and a bad course of action, between good qualities and bad qualities, between a right and a wrong way of doing things. It is simply that even though these differences clearly and distinctly exist, they are not to be taken as something intrinsic to the attributes, actions, or things involved. As a general rule, there are no attributes of the soul that are good or bad. One cannot determine that a given quality is always and with every person the same. In certain societies and cultures, love, pity, and compassion may be considered good; and yet there may also be occasions, outside these cultures and even within them, when these qualities could be considered bad, leading one astray into sadness or sin. Similarly, pride, selfishness, and even hate are not always bad attributes. As the sages have said, there is no attribute that lacks its injurious aspect, its negation and failure, just as there is no attribute—even if connected with doubt and heresy—that has not, under some circumstances, its holy aspect. From this point of view, the good and bad qualities are not set opposite one another, with love always on the side of the good and the other qualities always on the side of the bad. Rather all the attributes, all the emotions, and all the potentialities of the heart and personality are set on the same level and considered good or bad, not according to some judgment of their intrinsic worth, but according to the way they are used.

In Hebrew good attributes are called "good measures," which suggests that the excellence of a quality is determined by its proportion, not by its being what it is in itself, but by its properly related use in particular circumstances. Everything that is not in the right measure, that relates out of proportion to a situation, tends to be bad.

The good is thus that which is contained within proper limits, and the bad, that which breaks out and goes beyond these limits; and it does not matter whether this exceeding of boundaries is positive or negative, restrictive or excessive, whether refusal of affection or even generosity in love. And, in fact, this need for balance is true of every living organism; each cell in the organism has a certain form and a fixed rate of growth; and whenever its form is distorted or its growth exceeds what it should be, the result is pathology. The evil in the world is just such a bursting of bounds, that which allows for the existence of parasitic and injurious factors.

It is easy to confuse this principle of keeping within proper bounds with mediocrity, with being neither one thing nor another. In reality there is a vast difference. What the Jewish sages recommend is not only a middle way, it is a rejection of extremes in terms of a clear knowledge of how to keep everything, including the extreme, in its proper place. Consequently, in general, there are no preconceptions about what is the correct conduct for all situations, since the correctness of a way of being is itself only measurable in terms of a specific set of circumstances that may or may not recur. There is therefore no possibility of fixing a single standard of behavior. If anything is clear, it is that a rigid, unchanging way is wrong. Furthermore, this principle of movement, of constant change, is the principle manifested by the soul itself in its life on earth. To be sure, a person needs a special teacher or a great deal of guidance in order to be able always to find the right measure; usually choosing the correct way grows out of the soul's continual oscillation from one extreme to another. This pendulum swing of experience brings about a certain synthesis somewhere in the middle—although too often it is an artificial middle, merely halfway between good and evil and neither one nor the other.

The essence of life in the world, as formulated in Jewish writings, is exemplified by the terrible progress of the divine fire (Ezekiel 1) to and fro, up and back—the constant rhythm of the breath and the heart's blood. This principle of fluctuation seems even to be at the root of man's relation to Heaven and earth, evinced as the urge to extricate oneself from the bonds of matter and rise toward the Divine, and the equally urgent need to return to the world, with its problems, its substantiality, its life of sadness. To remain in any one condition of being, above or below, represents a cessation of effort, a dying, and therefore an evil. At times the yearning for Heaven is great enough to make one leave behind the world and everything in it; at other times the clutching at the earthly realities of action and the fulfillment of desire make one forget all else. This is not only a matter of periods in one's life; it is the very nature of life itself: in both the ascent to God and the descent to matter there is holiness. Never is any one way wholly sufficient unto itself, and it is only when they exist together that they constitute a real passage between Heaven and earth.

Similarly, there is no essential conflict or struggle in the opposition between mind and emotion, scholarship and faith, intellectual inquiry and simplicity of soul. The right way of life does not require a unity in this respect; on the contrary, it makes it obligatory to immerse oneself in the contradiction of these two approaches. A definite rhythm is established, with the regular daily alternation of study and prayer. The study of the Talmud and associated literature is basically intellectual and often rises to abstract thinking and even probes the nature of doubt. Prayer is an entirely different activity, with its own time set apart. It is an experience of feeling and devotion, a forgetting of all doubts and complaints in a simple earnestness, a purity of heart. A Jewish person is required to be in both these worlds, moving from the clarity and lucidity of a certain aspect of study of the Torah, which is almost blinding in its luminousness, to a critical and stubborn questioning of things that have no ultimate answer, and then on again to the realm of feeling and utmost devotion. The rhythmic oscillation is considered proper; to get stuck in any one aspect, whether it be study or devotion, is considered a grievous error.

With this unusual synthesis as a fundamental approach, Judaism has been able to develop two branches, which, from the outside, seem to be worlds apart and totally contradictory: the soaring power of prophecy and the careful performing of the *mitzvot* with precise attention to detail.

Jewish life and thought is not merely a reconciliation of these two; it lives in the rhythmic fluctuation between them as the only possible course of holiness. The essence of spirituality cannot be localized in either the wisdom of the intellect or the simplicity of the heart, being beyond all these; it can, however, be reached by the constancy of a struggle to overcome the contradiction. Indeed, the contradiction itself offers a passage from one world to another. As one transfers attention from the inwardness of prayer and yearning for the Divine to the outwardness of reason, study, and correct action, one becomes aware of the divine order of things, that everything has its proper place, measure, and time.

Indeed, the Jewish scriptures are full of this contradiction— as sharply emphasizing of the most minute detail as they are sublimely aware of the highest and most all-embracing truths, as ready to question everything as to accept without question. The Holy One is discovered to be beyond all this; He is immanent and flows within life, in the passage from one world to another, from one way of doing things to another, from one right measure of existence to the whole world of forms. Thus the possibilities of relating and responding to God are countless in number. There is no above or below in approaching Him, no preference between mind or feeling. On the contrary, in moving up and back from one such realm of experience to the other, its apparent opposite in life, one reaches a rhythm of being which is the life of holiness.

7

The Human Image

ONE OF THE THINGS THAT SHAPED the ritual forms of Judaism is the absolute prohibition against fashioning a statue or a mask. This prohibition goes back to the Second Commandment, forbidding the making of an image. It should be emphasized that this commandment was interpreted not as prohibiting the creation of any and every kind of picture or figure, but only as prohibiting an image that could in any way be used in ritual. The prohibition, then, covered not only the fashioning of a false god or an idolatrous object of worship but also any statue or image of the true God himself or of any of His angels, or even a statue (but not a painting) of the human figure.

On the surface, the prohibition simply reiterates the fundamental opposition to idolatry on all its levels. And in so doing it implies a repudiation of all material representation of the Divine in any form whatever. This prohibition may be better understood, however, in the context of its use in the terminology and expressions of prophecy. For not only the style of the prophets but the very nature of the Hebrew language itself leans away from the use of abstraction and prefers instead symbolic and figurative terms.

Thus the Bible and the other literary creations of the Jews, such as *Aggadah* and the Kabbalah, abound with anthropomorphisms of all kinds, not only in relation to the deity but in every sort of description. This humanization of the world's reality, both of the objects and creatures lower than man and of those higher, are among the profoundly consistent aspects of the use of the holy tongue. As one of the sages expressed it: The soul describes everything according to the configuration of its mansions, which is the body. In other words, the world is conceptualized and its objects described by a system of metaphors based on the human body. The language thus "raises the lowly" by images like "the head [top] of the mountain" and "the foot of the mountain"; and it "brings down the high" by descriptions such as the "seat" of the Almighty, the "hand" of God, the "eye" of the Lord, and the like.

This use of plastic imagery and symbols is so characteristic of the language that it is hard to find a sentence in the Scriptures that is not constructed on the basis of metaphorical description rather than of abstract conceptualization. Imagery-bound concepts are to be found everywhere, in almost every paragraph of the books of law and jurisprudence as well as in poetry and literature, and serve primarily, and most strikingly, to describe all that pertains to the holy.

Precisely because of this prevalence of metaphorical statement, and the widespread use of figures of speech drawn from the human image, it becomes all the more necessary to emphasize that they are allegorical truths and not actual descriptions of reality. For there was a certain danger that the word pictures, or imagistic descriptions, of sacred symbols in the Bible—and even more so in the Kabbalah—could lead to a crude material apprehension of the divine essence and of the higher reality. Hence the prohibition against all depiction of holiness through physical, plastic means. Accompanying it, and perhaps stemming from this extreme revulsion to plastic semblance of the Divine, Jewish tradition also maintains a certain suspicion of man's tendency to design, elaborate, and portray himself.

This inclination, to keep the greatest possible distance between man and God, has led to a more abstract comprehension of divine truth and of the ability to distinguish falsehood in the various descriptions of God. To be sure, there is a basic reason for the historical fact that the Jews, with their cultural or linguistic inclination to describe everything in terms of the human, shrink from depicting the spiritual in gross, physical terms. To understand this reason, a few points have to be elucidated. One has to recall that our whole material world is only a part of a greater system of worlds; whatever happens and offers itself to our apprehension is also tied in with that which is above and below our world.

Which is to say, the nonphysical essences of other worlds are projected into our material world, adjusting to its limits and to its physical time and space. Thus, despite the limits of our material world, the higher worlds are present in it and may even be distinguished in one form or another. Indeed, every detail of the material world is a kind of projection of a nonphysical reality that has chosen to reveal itself physically in this particular way.

In such a view of the world there is bound to be a double distortion. First, there is the distortion that results from the projection of something nonphysical on a physical reality: since in essence these two are so different, it is impossible for anything in our world to be a complete replica of a nonphysical reality. Then there is the distortion resulting from the fact that our world is no longer in its first stage of pristine purity and health. The various creatures in this world do what they have to do as best they can, thereby making certain changes in the structure of the world—the most auspicious changes and distortions, of course, being those that result from the actions of man.

By virtue of his free will and the ability to impose his will on other creatures in the material world, man is, to a certain degree, independent of the forces of the other worlds, higher and lower. Consequently the thoughts and actions of man, especially his sins and his mistakes, can derange the simpler forms of nature and the world and can even affect reality in other worlds.

This world is therefore no longer a true replica or a true projection of the higher worlds. Only in its original state, that of the Garden of Eden, was it structured as a more or less perfect duplication of the physical world and the spiritual worlds. Since then all the worlds, and our world in particular, have become increasingly distorted, and much of the original essence has changed in various ways. Only those persons who know the secret of existence in the universe can know the extent to which the duplication between the worlds still exists and can perceive the essential analogy between the physical world and the spiritual worlds. They can make out the hidden paths in the concrete reality of the world leading to the upper worlds, and they read into whatever is apprehended as real the symbols and models of a higher world taking us step by step upward to the very pinnacle and source of all the levels.

And just as all of the worlds are reflected, to some extent, in the physical world in which we live, so to an even greater extent—indeed, in principle up to the utmost heights of divine revelation—is the inner image of the worlds reflected in the image of man. To be sure, all the creatures in the world, the great and the small, constitute copies and symbols of aspects in the existences of higher worlds, but in man there is also reflected the relationships among various aspects of existence. Thus man is, on the one hand, a part of the general creation of the world, and on the other hand, as the possessor of the special attribute of free will, he is the unique concrete expression of divine reality in the worlds. For all the other worlds are ordered according to the fixed laws of cause and effect whether of a physical or a nonphysical nature. Only man can willfully change the framework somewhat and activate the "vicious circles" in various ways.

Therefore, man alone is the expression of the creative will in the world. By virtue of the spark that is his soul, man manifests the divine plenty existing in all the worlds unto their most sublime heights. So that the whole semblance of man is, in a certain sense, in the image of God. Which is to say, man is both the projection of the creative divine plenty into physical reality and the divine form revealed to the higher worlds as it appears in our world.

Clearly, the divine representation in man is far from complete; neither the body nor the soul of man faithfully expresses the supreme essence. And yet man, in all his spiritual and physical aspects, is to be viewed as a symbolic order oriented to the order of sovereignty in the world, the order of the ten *Sefirot* of the world of emanation.

One of the definitions of the name "Man" or "Adam" is likeness (*domeh*) to the Supreme. For, like God, man creates the worlds in the image of himself. His physical form, in the assemblage of its several parts, also constitutes a system that is a sort of model of the inner network of all the worlds. The structure of man is a paradigm of the structure of the worlds; it is the key to the order of the *mitzvot*; and it is also the configuration that symbolizes the system of relationships among the worlds. All of the organs of man correspond to higher essences in other worlds. The general structure of the human body is homologous with the order of the ten *Sefirot*, every part of the body of a man being congruous with a particular *Sefirah*.

Thus when the prophets speak of the "hand" or the "eyes" of the Lord, it is understood that they are not speaking of essences in any way physically similar to the human hand or eye. At the same time there *is* some essential connection to the body of man. The relation between the right hand and the left hand, for instance, is a matter of a profound principle, which is derived from the difference between the *Sefirot* of *Hesed* and *Gevurah*. And so, too, with all the parts of the human body, in their general configuration and down to the smallest detail.

Man may therefore be viewed as a symbol or a model of the divine essence, his entire outer and inner structure manifesting relationships and different aspects existing in that supreme essence.

The secret of the positive *mitzvot*, the commandments to perform certain actions, lies, in a manner of speaking, in the activization of the limbs of the body, in certain movements and certain ways of doing things which are congruous with higher realities and higher relationships in other worlds. In fact, every movement, every gesture, every habitual pattern, and every isolated act that man does with his body has an effect in whole systems of essences in other dimensions with and against one another.

Clearly, an ordinary person does not know anything of this; at best he is conscious only to a very small degree of the things he does and of their higher significance. Even among those few who are able to unravel the riddle and know the meaning of these secrets, only select individuals reach that state of being where knowledge is automatically lived out and manifested. It is a state where every act of a *mitzvah* or an impulsive movement or a dance, expresses, knowingly and unknowingly, the higher relationships—following on analogous parts of the body, in their separate as well as in their total effects.

Thus, it may be understood why fashioning and exhibiting the image of a man was also prohibited. Since man was, according to one of the sages, "an effigy of the king," anyone who tried to make something in his image was creating a statue, an idol. For man was supposed to know that his body was not only the temple and the abode of the soul, but in itself an expression of the supreme essence; and therefore he had to maintain a special relation to the body, acknowledging that its gestures, movements, and actions involved manifestations of the higher order.

Since, like his soul, the body of man is oriented to higher essences, the idiom of the Kabbalah often makes use of organs of the body to depict conditions and higher relations in other worlds. In practical kabbalistic works there are to be found indications of various, sometimes impossible, movements of the limbs and parts of the body which serve to shed light on the complex occult ways of the Chariot on different planes and in different worlds.

And as has been said, precisely because there is such a voluminous and frequent use of symbolic structures and models, most of them connected with external forms, it is necessary to be extremely cautious about any attempt to give a concrete physical interpretation to higher essences.

From all of which it may be understood why, in actual fact, there is no Jewish iconography to speak of. True, in the Holy Temple there were a few symbolic elements—not images of the Holy One, Blessed be He, but of the cherubin who bear the Chariot. Even these symbols were hidden away in the inner recesses of the Temple, so that they should not become part of the ritual—for it has often happened in history that things once having no more than a symbolic or reminiscence value have been turned into ritual objects or idolatrous worship. That is why throughout the generations Jewish tradition has stringently resisted anything like defined iconographic imagery.

Instead, the tradition developed the whole order of *mitzvot*, which may be seen as a stylization of a system of pictures and symbols using the body and mind of man. For in a certain sense, the *mitzvot*, in all their minutiae, constitute an endless, moving series of images depicting a vision of supreme revelation. These images are expressed in the objective actions but are not to be identified with them; and if the action is a correct action in terms of the original revelation, then it will have significance within other systems of reality. Thus, precisely because the whole world is so full of symbols and meanings, pictures and forms, there is a repudiation of any attempt to make any one special image; for the existing reality is itself so entirely made up of, and by, one single organized picture.

This grasp of symbols, then, applies not only to the human figure but to every reality in the world. To those who know this meaning, reality is more clear and comprehensible. Thus, for instance, there is significance to the various colors and their relationships, each one expressing a certain *Sefirah*; fruits and flowers, kinds of living creatures, forms of vegetable life and minerals, all have individual meaning and at the same time make up a great unified system in which the whole of reality acts and is acted upon; and this is the vast picture, the great work of plastic art of a moment in time.

In Jewish thought, the concept of beauty is linked to the central *Sefirah* of *Tiferet* which in itself is actually an expression of several basic elements of existence, each of them manifesting the same fundamental quality in different ways such as: truth, Torah, beauty, compassion. The common denominator may be seen as harmony. And since this apprehension of harmony is so many-sided and variegated, it cannot be reduced to only one aesthetic meaning. Even in the Hebrew language there is a constant interchange and substitution between the concepts of the good and the beautiful, the good being called beautiful and the beautiful good, because both are grasped as a harmony between things. *Tiferet* is thus the basis of the good, the beautiful, and the true, without ever being manifested or capable of being directly expressed in an "image."

8

Repentance

REPENTANCE IS ONE of the ultimate spiritual realities at the core of Jewish faith. Its significance goes far beyond the narrow meaning of contrition or regret for sin, and it embraces a number of concepts considered to be fundamental to the very existence of the world.

Certain sages go so far as to include repentance among the entities created before the world itself. The implication of this remarkable statement is that repentance is a universal, primordial phenomenon; in such a context it has two meanings. One is that it is embedded in the root structure of the world; the other, that before man was created, he was given the possibility of changing the course of his life. In this latter sense repentance is the highest expression of man's capacity to choose freely—it is a manifestation of the divine in man. Man can extricate himself from the binding web of his life, from the chain of causality that otherwise compels him to follow a path of no return.

Repentance also comprises the notion that man has a measure of control over his existence in all dimensions, including time. Time flows in one direction; it is impossible to undo or even to alter an action after it has occurred and become an "event," an objective fact. However, even though the past is "fixed," repentance admits of an ascendancy over it, of the possibility of changing its significance in the context of the present and future. This is why repentance has been presented as something created before the world itself. In a world of the inexorable flow of time, in which all objects and events are interconnected in a relationship of cause and effect, repentance is the exception: it is the potential for something else.

The Hebrew word for repentance, *Teshuvah*, has three different though related meanings. First, it denotes "return," a going back to God or to the Jewish faith. Second, it can mean "turning about" or "turning to," adopting another orientation or direction in life. Third, *Teshuvah* signifies "response."

The root meaning is return to God, or to Judaism, in the inclusive sense of embracing in faith, thought, and deed. On the simplest, most literal level, the possibility of return can only exist for someone who was once "there," such as an adult who retains childhood memories or other recollections of Jewish life. But is it not possible for someone to return who was never "there," who has no memories of a Jewish way of life, for whom Judaism is not a personal but a historical or biological heritage, or no more than an epithet that gives him a certain meaningless identity? The answer is unequivocally in the affirmative, for—on the more profound level—repentance as return reaches beyond such personal configurations. It is indeed a return to Judaism, but not to the external framework, not to the religious norms that man seeks to understand or to integrate into, with their clear-cut formulae, directives, actions, and rituals; it is a return to one's own paradigm, to the prototype of the Jewish person. Intellectually, this paradigm may be perceived as a historical reality to which one is personally related, but beyond this is the memory of the essential archetype that is a part of the soul structure of the individual Jew. In spite of the vast range of ways in which a Jew can alienate himself from his past and express himself in foreign cultural forms, he nevertheless retains a metaphysically, almost genetically, imprinted image of his Jewishness. To use a metaphor from the world of botany: a change of climate, soil, or other physical conditions can induce marked alterations in the form and the functioning of a plant, and even the adoption of characteristics of other species and genera, but the unique paradigm or prototype persists.

Reattachment to one's prototype may be expressed in many ways, not only in accepting a faith or a credo or in fulfilling certain traditional obligations. As he liberates himself from alien influences, the penitent can only gradually straighten himself out; he has to overcome the forms engraved by time and place before he can reach his own image. He must break free of the chains, the limitations, and the restrictions imposed by environment and education. If pursued aimlessly, with no clear goal, this primal search does not transcend the urge to be free; without a vector, it can be spiritually exhausting and may never lead to a genuine discovery of the true self. In this respect, not in vain has the Torah been perceived as a system of knowledge and insights that guide the individual Jew to reach his own pattern of selfhood. The mutual relationship between the individual Jew and Judaism, between the man and his God, depends on the fact that Judaism is not only the Law, the prescribed religious practice, but is a life framework that embraces his entire existence; furthermore, it is ultimately the only framework in which, in his aloneness and in his search, he will be able to find himself. Whereas potentially a man can adapt himself, there exists, whether he acknowledges it or not, a path that is his own, which relates to him, to his family, to his home.

Repentance is a complex process. Sometimes a man's entire life is no more than an ongoing act of repentance on several levels. It his been said that a man's path of spiritual development, whether he has sinned or not, is in a certain sense a path of repentance. It is an endeavor to break away from the past and reach a higher level. However, notwithstanding the complexity and the deeply felt difficulties involved, there is a clear simplicity in the elemental point that is the point of the turning.

Remoteness from God is, of course, not a matter of physical distance, but a spiritual problem of relationship. The person who is not going along the right path is not farther away from God but is, rather, a man whose soul is oriented toward and relating with other objects. The starting point of repentance is precisely this fulcrum point upon which a person turns himself about, away from the pursuit of what he craves, and confronts his desire to approach God; this is the moment of conversion, the crucial moment of repentance.

It should be noted that generally this does not occur at a moment of great self-awareness. Though a person may be acutely conscious of the moment of repentance, the knowledge can come later. It is in fact rare for repentance to take the form of a sudden, dramatic conversion, and it generally takes the form of a series of small turnings.

Irrespective of the degree of awareness, several spiritual factors come together in the process of conversion. Severance is an essential factor. The repentant cuts himself off from his past, as though saying: "Everything in my life up to this point is now alien to me; chronologically or historically it may be part of me—but I no longer accept it as such." With a new goal in life, a person assumes a new identity. Aims and aspirations are such major expressions of the personality that renouncing them amounts to a severance of the old self. The moment of turning thus involves not only a change of attitude, but also a metamorphosis. When the process is fully realized, it includes a departure from, a rejection of, and a regret for the past, and an acceptance, a promise of change in the future. The sharper the turning, the more deeply conscious it is, the more prominent will these aspects be—a shaking free of the past, a transfiguration of self, and an eager thrust forward into a new identity.

Repentance also includes the expectance of a response, of a confirmation from God that this is indeed the way, that this is the direction. Nevertheless, the essence of repentance is bound up more with turning than with response. When response is direct and immediate, the process of repentance cannot continue, because it has in a way arrived at its goal; whereas one of its essential components is an increase of tension, the tension of the ongoing experience and of yearning. As long as the act of repentance lasts, the seeking for response continues, and the soul still strives to receive from elsewhere the answer, the pardon.

Response is not always given; and even when it is, it is not the same for every man. Repentance is a gradual process: final response is awarded not to specific isolated acts but to the whole; the various components, the desire to act, the performing of the deed based on anticipation, the yearning, disappointment, and hope, are rewarded, if at all, by partial answers. In other words, a response to turning is given to a man as "something on account," the rest to be paid out later. A person generally hears the longed-for answer not when he puts his question, not when he is struggling, but when he pauses on a summit and looks back on his life.

Jewish thought pays little attention to inner tranquility and peace of mind. The feeling of "behold, I've arrived" could well undermine the capacity to continue, suggesting as it does that the Infinite can be reached in a finite number of steps. In fact, the very concept of the Divine as infinite implies an activity that is endless, of which one must never grow weary. At every rung of his ascent, the penitent, like any person who follows the way of God, perceives mainly the remoteness. Only in looking back can one obtain some idea of the distance already covered, of the degree of progress. Repentance does not bring a sense of serenity or of completion but stimulates a reaching out in further effort. Indeed, the power and the potential of repentance lie in increased incentive and enhanced capacity to follow the path even farther. The response is often no more than an assurance that one is in fact capable of repenting, and its efficacy lies in the growing awareness, with time, that one is indeed progressing on the right path. In this manner the conditions are created in which repentance is no longer an isolated act but has become a permanent possibility, a constant process of going toward. It is a going that is both the rejection of what was once axiomatic and an acceptance of new goals.

The paths of the penitent and of the man who has merely lost his direction differ only in terms of the aim, not in going itself. The Jewish approach to life considers the man who has stopped going—he who has a feeling of completion, of peace, of a great light from above that has brought him to rest—to be someone who has lost his way. Only he whom the light continues to beckon, for whom the light is as distant as ever, only he can be considered to have received some sort of response. The path a man has taken is revealed to him only in retrospect, in a contemplation of the past that grants confidence in what lies ahead. This awareness is in fact the reward, and it is conditional on the continuation of the return.

The essence of repentance has frequently been found in the poetic lines of the Song of Songs, "The King had brought me to his chambers [1:4]." This verse has been interpreted as meaning that he whose search has reached a certain level feels that he is in the palace of the King. He goes from room to room, from hall to hall, seeking Him out. However, the King's palace is an endless series of worlds, and as a man proceeds in his search from room to room, he holds only the end of the string. It is, nevertheless, a continuous going, a going after God, a going to God, day after day, year after year.

Repentance is not just a psychological phenomenon, a storm within a human teacup, but is a process that can effect real change in the world, in all the worlds. Every human action elicits certain inevitable results that extend beyond their immediate context, passing from one level of existence to another, from one aspect of reality to another. The act of repentance is, in the first place, a severance of the chain of cause and effect in which one transgression follows inevitably upon another. Beyond this, it is an attempt to nullify and even to alter the past. This can be achieved only when man, subjectively, shatters the order of his own existence. The thrust of repentance is to break through the ordinary limits of the self. Obviously, this cannot take place within the routine of life, but it can be an ongoing activity throughout life. Repentance is thus something that persists; it is an ever-renewed extrication from causality and limitation.

When man senses the wrongness, evil, and emptiness in his life, it is not enough that he yearn for God or try to change his way of life. Repentance is more than aspiration and yearning, for it also involves the sense of despair. And it is this very despair—and, paradoxically, the sin that precedes it—that gives man the possibility of overleaping his past. The desperation of the endeavor to separate himself from his past, to reach heights that the innocent and ordinary man is not even aware of, gives the penitent the power to break the inexorability of his fate, sometimes in a way that involves a total destruction of his past, his goals, and almost all of his personality.

Nevertheless, this level of repentance is only a beginning, for all of the penitent's past actions continue to operate: the sins he committed and the injuries he inflicted exist as such in time. Even though the present has been altered, earlier actions and their consequences continue to generate a chain of cause and effect. The significance of the past can be changed only at the higher level of repentance called *Tikkun*.

The first stage in the process of *Tikkun* is of equilibration. For every wrong deed in his past, the penitent is required to perform certain acts that surpass what is demanded of an "ordinary" individual, to complement and balance the picture of his life. He must build and create anew and change the order of good and evil in such a way that not only his current life activity acquires new form and direction, but the totality of his life receives a consistently positive value.

The highest level of repentance, however, lies beyond the correction of sinful deeds and the creation of independent, new patterns that counterweigh past sins and injuries; it is reached when the change and the correction penetrate the very essence of the sins once committed and, as the sages say, create the condition in which a man's transgressions become his merits: This level of *Tikkun* is reached when a person draws from his failings not only the ability to do good, but the power to fall again and again and, notwithstanding, to transform more extensive and important segments of life. It is using the knowledge of the sin of the past and transforming it into such an extraordinary thirst for good that it becomes a divine force. The more a man was sunk in evil, the more anxious he becomes for good. This level of being, in which failings no longer exert a negative influence on the penitent, in which they no longer reduce his stature or sap his strength, but serve to raise him, to stimulate his progress—this is the condition of genuine *Tikkun*.

Thus the complete correction of past evil cannot be brought about merely by acknowledgment of wrong and contrition; indeed, this acknowledgment often leads, in practice, to a loss of incentive, a state of passivity, of depression; furthermore, the very preoccupation with memories of an evil impulse may well revive that impulse's hold on a person. In genuine *Tikkun*, everything that was once invested in the forces of evil is elevated to receive another meaning within a new way of life; deeds once performed with a negative intention are transformed into a completely new category of activity. To be sure, forces of evil that had parasitically attached themselves to a person are not easily compelled to act in the direction of the good. Spiritual possibilities of which a man who has not sinned can never even gain an awareness have to emerge and become a driving force.

The penitent thus does more than return to his proper place. He performs an act of amendment of cosmic significance; he restores the sparks of holiness which had been captured by the powers of evil. The sparks that he had dragged down and attached to himself are now raised up with him, and a host of forces of evil return and are transformed to forces of good. This is the significance of the statement in the Talmud that in the place where a completely repentant person stands, even the most saintly cannot enter; because the penitent has at his disposal not only the forces of good in his soul and in the world, but also those of evil, which he transforms into essences of holiness.

9

The Search for Oneself

THROUGHOUT LIFE ONE ASKS the same question in many forms. This question lies at the heart of a search for oneself, a search that begins with the first glimmer of consciousness and continues to the very last breath. For every human being it varies, and at every stage of his life. Often the search is conducted without any intellectual comprehension of what one is about. Sometimes the subtlest philosophical nuances of thought and speculation may be brought into play, and at others the question does not even rise to consciousness. But one never really extricates oneself from the context of the issue, Who am I? And from its corollaries: Where do I come from? Where am I going? What for? Why?

One's first thoughts, even in infancy, are attempts to probe the limits and distinctions of the self as against those of the world. Later, the same riddle of existence assumes innumerable disguises—even the disguise of simplicity, when the answer seems to lie in the palm of one's hand and the problem barely seems worth bothering with, although even then the question persists subconsciously and works its effect deviously. Virtually all of the investigation a person ever does, whether of himself or of problems outside himself, consists for the most part of pyramids upon pyramids of answers to that basic question about the essence of his being.

To be sure, it takes both time and considerable introspection to get beyond the elaborate mental constructions, the words and ideas, devised by everyone. Often, too, a person will feel that he can make do with partial pragmatic answers, that he has as much as he can handle just coping with the necessities of the everyday. In this way, he evades the primary question, even though an answer to it could supply meaning to everything else. Because in addition to being primary and natural, the question of identity is also threatening, and not only stirs a vast number of possible answers but offers a glimpse into an abyss of yet further, and unanswerable, questions. So it is that people so frequently speed up their pace in the race to achieve the things they desire, and find themselves running away from the question of why, of who is so desperately pursuing these desires.

Even though the question of the self is one that has since the beginning of time been contemplated by many profound minds, it is not really a philosophical problem. Philosophical, psychological, or scientific treatment of it only provides different frameworks and forms of expressions for answers that are in any case continuously being proven inadequate. Philosophy, psychology, science, all merely isolate the basic problem within an observable small field where it can in turn be broken down into secondary problems, every one of which may, by itself, be important and certainly interesting but, taken together, nevertheless seem far removed from any truly satisfactory response to the question of one's place in the world. Such a response can come only from within. It cannot be supplied within any other frame of reference or merely by ideas or symbols.

The question appears in the very first story of the Bible—the story of Adam and Eve. After committing their primal sin, they are frightened and hide themselves among the trees of the garden. The voice of God is heard calling unto Adam: Where art thou? This question, like the entire tale, is emblematic of human life. If only man as an individual, if only the race of man as a whole, were able to foreswear the sin of the Tree of Knowledge—the sin of "knowing," for which there is no real corresponding need in the soul—he would perhaps also avoid the sin of responding to the question before it has arisen: when man knows more than he needs to know, when what he learns are no more than fragments of information, heaps of unrelated facts which, whether they are correct or incorrect, become a barrier to experience itself. Were it not for the obfuscation inevitable in the formulation of answers without questions—that is, answers without inner immediate meaning—man might, like other creatures, have been able to feel the essence of himself more clearly and simply; there would be no problem about the direction he has to take. His instinctual makeup, the elementary existence in him, would guide him to finding his place in the world and to his understanding of himself. But after the sin of knowingness, the luminous simplicity of his way is lost to him. He does indeed gain the power of doubt and uncertainty, but he loses the primal feeling of his place and position. And therefore the questions—it is one question really—with which a man begins are not the one he might have dared to ask in purity: Where am I? Where am I going? What am I doing? This question he hears, not from within but from without, as the voice of God asking Adam what he does not dare to ask himself: Where art thou? And thus he may repeat to himself: Indeed, where am I? The only thing he can say with any degree of certainty is that he has lost his way and is hiding; he cannot say anything more positive. The point is that the consequence of sin, whether experienced directly or indirectly in the guise of open or repressed guilt feelings, is that man hides himself from God, that the place he happens to be is a hiding place, and in order for him to move at all he has to hear the question, Where? Where are you? The voice in the garden is still reverberating throughout the world, and it is still heard, not always openly, or in full consciousness but nevertheless still heard in one way or another, in a person's soul. Even when one is totally ignorant of the fact that the voice is the voice of God, one can nevertheless frequently hear what it says: Where are you? Where am I? The question can be invoked in full consciousness and, on the other hand, can also come to a person not only when he is hiding from God, but even when he does not know that he is hiding from Him. The question can present itself to someone hopelessly without aim or purpose, just as it can haunt someone who imagines that everything is clear and understandable to him. To anyone, at any time whatever, the question may be flung: Where are you?

What is more, in being aware that the question is asked of one, there is a still deeper significance, so inwardly subtle that not everyone discerns it. The person really listening to the question, or to life's echo of it, may, in his attentiveness and in his reflection on what he hears, be able to discern not only the elemental issue but even the voice of the one asking the question. In other words, this question about where I am in my world is outwardly one that a person can ask of himself, but inwardly it is the voice of God speaking to man: to man who has lost his way. And the moment a person reaches this awareness, he can grasp something which, with all the pain of the question, with all the fearful terror and awe of an encounter with God, leads to that which is larger and more glorious. For the question of where I am—the question of a man who confronts himself alone, even if he is within a family, a community, a nation, and even if he feels at home in the world—this utterly solitary question is fundamentally resolved at the moment when a person realizes that it is the other side of the question God asks of man: Where are you? This, then, is the response to despair, to the unanswered plea of the bereaved and bewildered, to the lost son who cannot find a home. It is the Other Voice asking the very same question.

The search for the self, in other words, the search for the essence, the inwardness, and the way of the soul, stems from the recognition that one is alone in the world. When man stands suddenly alone in the world, when everything seems to be addressed only to him, then there is no aspect of reality that does not challenge him. He has to relate to this person or that situation, he has to judge and resolve all the problems of the world with himself as its center. It would appear that the real agony begins when one's horizons in this world expand, as one rises from one level to another, and as one's intellect and imagination encompass more of the domain of the human. With external reality pressing heavily on man, the physical, the philosophical, the psychological questions only intensify the urgency of the basic question of the self. Man may thus deepen his inner essence in his solitariness, making it something quite separate and special, adding new powers and talents, new ways of seeing things, sometimes also a deepening of thought, and sometimes nobility of spirit. And yet very often it seems that the basic point, the self, is untouched—even though the more a person grows, the more the problem of the self should also grow. So it is that a certain depth is added to the solitary person; he finds a whole world of inner treasures and spiritual powers. These can occupy the mind and give one the feeling of connection with things, even if only for a time. But ultimately the things that such a person attempts to cling to as moorings, as fixed points, are over and over again revealed as delusory. It is not that real points do not exist in the world, but rather that they are not permanent. A man cannot build on them and relate to them as to something fixed and definite, because in the long run all these points, both in external space and in his interior depths, only refer in turn to one focal point, to that very self which has no anchor at all.

The seeker is caught in a paradox. He is dismayed to learn that the resolution of the search for the self is not to be found by going into the self, that the center of the soul is to be found not in the soul but outside of it, that the center of gravity of existence is outside of existence. He may, to be sure, experience a glimmer of hope when he discovers that the focal point of individual existence can be found in existence as a whole. This discovery will bring him to what is stated in Psalm 73: "My flesh and my hearth faileth: but God is the strength of my heart and my portion forever." He becomes aware, in other words, that the center of being is in God and not in man. Only the point to be found at the center of the absolute provides the basis for a meaningful answer to the question that appears at first to be so very simple and so very distant from the search for the absolute.

A person may therefore stray as far as possible, infinitely far, from God, and there he can find the source of his deepest self, the point of the meaning of his soul. He orients himself on the map of his world and is startled and pained to learn that he is not necessarily its center. But recognizing that he is part of a larger existence that does go to the heart of the world, he can begin to take the path to this existence.

Sometimes it may seem to a person that in such a position—not at the center but as a point on the periphery of himself, seeing his soul not as the first and the last of everything but as a flash of the infinite light—he is losing himself, losing his freedom and independence. This is not so, of course. His previous sense of his existence, that he was its hero and king and god, is, besides being something of a sacrilege, an empty shell without content. Defining oneself only in relation to secondary things leaves one's being as nothing but a series of empty shells each dependent on the others for meaning. Thus a man is defined as this one's friend, that one's son, the father of another, the one occupied with this or that, the one who thinks this or that, someone engaged with certain problems, and all these are only shadow relationships that leave him a faceless, empty figure trying to clothe itself with some visible individuation. Only when a man can relate his inner center to God as the first and foremost and only reality, only then does his self take on meaning. It ceases to be a relative entity without any content of its own and becomes itself a significant content.

Here we have what is perhaps the second paradox of the search for self, that only by ceasing to see oneself as a supremely independent essence can one say with all sincerity, This is where I am. It is the self-obliterating view of oneself that provides the true basis of all existence, that makes possible a firm grasp of the truth of reality. For then the circumscribing immensities of existence take shape in one's understanding, and it becomes apparent that one is a part of them.

One becomes conscious of a vast arc, curving from the divine source to oneself, which corresponds to the question, Where do I come from? while at the same time a line curving from oneself to Him corresponds to the question, Where am I going? And within this great circle, which includes all the levels of man, each person can discover the special lines of his own direction—which again, are not simply random points in reality but are the expressions of his individual personality, the shape of his soul. Because even when all the souls flow in and out of the same primal source, and all similarly aspire to reach out and grow and return to this source, even then, the way of every soul—for all it has in common with and resembles all the others—is unique unto itself and justifies its separate existence. Myriads of sparks reflect the primal light, every one of them with its own situation and its own set of circumstances.

When a man learns that just as he broods over himself so does God yearn for him and look for him, he is at the beginning of a higher level of consciousness. From this moment he can begin to follow the guiding strings that are leading him, usually with enormous toil and labor, toward the focal point of himself. For in truth it is not one question with two sides but a meeting place of two questions, that of man seeking himself and of God seeking man. Together they can approach a solution of the problem of man's existence. And in the search for this solution, within this desperate exploration, this going after God, a man will rediscover himself as well as the definition of his own particular being.

10

Mitzvot

THE JEWISH WAY OF LIFE, or the way of life of a Jew who lives according to the Torah, is held to be extremely difficult. According to tradition there are said to be six hundred and thirteen commandments in the Torah. This, however, is misleading in a number of respects. For one thing, many of the positive commandments—that is, *mitzvot* that obligate one to perform certain actions—along with many of the prohibitions, are not actually concerned with life but refer either to the general structure of the whole of the Torah or to the Jewish nation as a body. No Jew, therefore, can be expected to keep all of the *mitzvot*. Actually, only a small number of the *mitzvot* relate to daily life, though if one adds to the formal list of *mitzvot* all the minute details that are not specifically included, one arrives at a sum of not hundreds but thousands of things that are to be done at certain times and certain places and in a special way. Indeed, seen as separate and unrelated commandments, each as an individual obligation and burden, these ancillary *mitzvot* seem to be a vast and even an absurd assortment of petty details which are, if not downright intimidating, then at least troublesome. What we call details, however, are only parts of greater units which in turn combine in various ways into a single entity. It is as though in examining the leaves and flowers of a tree, one were to be overwhelmed by the abundance, the variety, and the complexity of detail; but when one realizes that it is all part of the same single growth, all part of the same branching out into manifold forms of the one tree, then the details would cease to be disturbing and would be accepted as intrinsic to the wondrousness of the whole.

A basic idea underlying Jewish life is that there are no special frameworks for holiness. A man's relation to God is not set apart on a higher plane, not relegated to some special corner of time and place with all the rest of life taking place somewhere else. The Jewish attitude is that life in all its aspects, in its totality, must somehow or other be bound up with holiness. This attitude is expressed in part through conscious action: that is, through the utterance of prescribed prayers and blessings and following prescribed forms of conduct; and, in part, by adhering to a number of prohibitions.

Man generally passes through the world aware that it is full of possible colors and meanings; and he tries to make his own connection with all its many possibilities. What he may be less aware of is the fact that there are worlds upon worlds, besides the one he knows, dependent on his actions. In Judaism man is conceived, in all the power of his body and soul, as the central agent, the chief actor on a cosmic stage; he functions, or performs, as a prime mover of worlds, being made in the image of the Creator. Everything he does constitutes an act of creation, both in his own life and in other worlds hidden from his sight.

Every single particle of his body and every nuance of his thought and feeling are connected with forces of all kinds in the cosmos, forces without number; so that the more conscious he is of this order of things, the more significantly does he function as a Jewish person.

The system of the *mitzvot* constitutes the design for a coherent harmony, its separate components being like the instruments of an orchestra. So vast is the harmony to be created by this orchestra that it includes the whole world and promises the perfecting of the world. Seeing the *mitzvot* in this light, one may understand on the one hand, the need for so great a number of details and, on the other, the denial of any exclusive emphasis on any one detail or aspect of life. The *mitzvot* as a system include all of life, from the time one opens one's eyes in the morning until one goes to sleep, from the day of birth to the last breath.

Nevertheless, for practical purposes the system of *mitzvot* may be divided into several main fields: prayer and blessing; modes of conducting oneself on special days in the week or in the year; dietary regulations, such as permitted and forbidden foods; sexual behavior; relations to one's fellow man.

Daily life is marked off by three principal sessions of prayer. The prescribed body of prayer is, except for minor differences, the same for each session. *Shaharit*, the morning prayer, is recited before all activity is begun; the *Minha* afternoon prayer, before the sun sets; and the *Maariv* evening prayer, in the night. The times fixed for these prayers are intended not only to coincide with the changing of the day, but also to make response to subtle differences between the hours of the rising light, the declining light, and the actual darkness. The prayers are also related to the practical concerns of man, from the morning's preparation, in spiritual terms, for the activities of the day, to the late afternoon when man completes the tasks of the day and, still immersed in the day, is reminded that even in these hours he has to renew the contact with holiness. The evening prayer, recited at the end of the day's work, prepares one for making a reckoning with the soul and for rest.

The morning prayer, with its requirement that one don phylacteries and its additional selections for reciting, lasts longer than the others. The liturgy as a whole reflects the historic development of the Jewish people, every period adding something of its own. As a result, besides long selections from the Bible, the order of prayers contains verses and prayers from the time of the Second Temple and the generations following, up to and including the Middle Ages and even beyond. Basically, these prayers have a double significance, national and personal. They are for the most part general, rather than the supplications of a person in trouble. A person in need, of course, turns to the source of holiness with his own particular request or thanksgiving, but the liturgy as a whole simply provides for the participation of the individual in the prayers of the people. Therefore the prayers have a fixed order and wording and are generally spoken in the plural. At the same time, within the arrangement there is offered a prayer, a verse, or a sentence or even a whole order of prayers which express an individual's feelings at a particular moment. In the praying itself there is a kind of unification of all the souls present; the people taking part seem to become aware of one another and concerned about one another, just as there is verbalized expression of concern for the general welfare. Thus the individual who prays can, if he wishes, introduce a personal theme into the fixed liturgy which is intentionally open enough to allow everyone to express himself. Personal prayers are not supposed to be spontaneous outbursts of emotion, and indeed there is no place for such outbursts. There is a time set aside and a special formulation for personal prayer; and whenever one wishes, one can do so. The traditional liturgy is a repetitive exercise for the soul, fixed by a carefully selective process determined upon by the people as a collective entity over the centuries. It includes various meditation exercises before and during prayer and constitutes a way to rise in consciousness within a controlled situation. Thus prayer is not only an articulation of certain words but also a key and a sort of ladder on which a person may reach from level to level, if indeed he lends himself to the prayer according to its essence.

In addition to these prayers, whose contents are more or less fixed, there are many blessings. These are generally quite short, no more than reminders to a person that the actions he is taking are not just movements without meaning, but that they have significance and content. Such a blessing is recited before almost every *mitzvah* and also before almost every enjoyment that one experiences in the world, whether food and drink, smell, or pleasurable sights of all sorts. In fact, the task of the blessing is to remind one, to halt the process of habit and routine which draws man always into the realm of the mechanical and meaningless, and to set up at every moment of change in the flow of life the brief declaration that this particular thing one is doing is not for one's self or of one's self, but that at some point it is connected with a higher world. By these blessings, then, scattered throughout the entire day, in all manner of situations, one attains to an integration of the ordinary, habitual elements of life with a higher order of sanctity.

Besides the weekdays with their own round of daily prayer, there are the larger cycles of the week, the month, and the year, each with its special days: Sabbaths, festivals, and days of remembrance. The days of remembrance are usually holy days, fast days recalling distressing events in the nation's history, or joyful days to commemorate miracles and acts of divine grace. The central pillars in the structure of Jewish time, however, are the Sabbaths and the holidays written about in the Torah itself. The theme of these days and their special quality is a certain festive tranquility; they are days of absolute rest from work and activity of all kinds.

The Sabbath, with its severe prohibitions against all work, is actually connected with the process of Creation. Just as the creation of the world took place in six stages, six days of forming the things that comprise the physical world, so are the six days devoted to working on the material world, repairing it, building it up, raising it to a higher level; and the Sabbath that follows is again a return to the life within oneself—a return, like that of the Creator himself, to the higher worlds, the spiritual essences, the changeless source of all change. For being in the image of God, man must continue to carry or to supplement and to repair the original Creation and then retreat into himself, withdrawing from physical creativity and renewing the holiness that comes from rest and complete peace.

The *Halakhah*, the formal structure defining the order of *mitzvot*, prescribes in great detail the many things one is forbidden to do on the Sabbath. All of them, however, are derived from the same basic idea: that the Sabbath is the day when one ceases to be a creator in the domain of the outer world and turns inward toward holiness. This dual quality of the day, in which one is not only to refrain from creativity but also to complete creativity in spiritual terms, follows of course from this idea. So that *Tikkun*—putting the world in order, even the correcting of one's own soul, or healing its wounds—is not for the Sabbath. The Sabbath is to be made available for a summation of the things acquired during the week, in an attempt to raise them spiritually, and knowingly or unknowingly to bring the week to a greater harmony, to a higher level of perfection. Thus the Sabbath is the completion, or the crowning, of the week, when all that was done of a material and spiritual nature during the previous six days is summed up and enjoyed: that is to say, it is brought to a higher level of consecration in order that again in the following week there will be another rise in the same cycle of days.

The same insistence on rest and repudiation of everyday activity is true also for the holidays, even though these feast days do not contain the same profound idea of imitating the divine process of Creation in the cycle of one week. Still, they are bound up with the cycle of the year, the annual memorials of historic events in the nation's history which is also the divine history of mankind. Certain allowances are made to ease the sabbatical strictness of the feast days; nevertheless, the tendency is to go inward. Every holiday has its own particular quality, its own essence and spirituality, so that the way it is celebrated and the whole attitude of the soul toward it is different. The annual cycle goes from Passover, the memorial day for the beginning of the life of the soul and for the life of the nation, through the feast of *Shavuot*, the time of overcoming resistance and obstacles and the commemoration of the receiving of the Torah, which is the standing forth before the Supreme, until the feast of *Succot*, which is the time of ripening and maturity and reward.

The Day of Atonement, which is also numbered among the holidays, is a special day. Although a fast day, it is also the Sabbath of Sabbaths, embodying a moment in time that is even beyond the Sabbath. It is that day in the year which brings forth atonement, when the lower human world again rises, not only above the cycle of physical life but also, in a certain sense, above the all-embracing factors determining everything in an individual's own existence. It is the day on which nothing is done because creativity has been halted in the world; it is the day on which nothing is eaten or drunk because primordially man then comes out of the womb of the world to another realm, and only in this standing forth of man, which is his final release from toil and his exit from the world, does he make contact with that which is beyond the world, with the Divine, with the Absolute, by the side of whom he is able to move beyond the frontiers of the past, beyond the deeds he has done and the life he has lived, and attain to a higher stage of being and find rest and renewal on the plane of divine forgiveness.

And again, all the holidays, festivals, and memorials have many features, often seen as difficult restrictions or customs, each one of which grows organically out of the fundamental idea of the sacred day to which it belongs. Thus, in order for a person to gain the benefit of the special day, he must concentrate his energies and focus his consciousness on this significant idea and its symbolic representations; he has to attune himself to catch its resonance. The numerous and various details of the commandments then cease to be burdensome and are accepted wholly as an outer expression, the clear and specified relationship of the person with the fundamental spiritual experience.

The *mitzvot* and the *halakhot* pertaining to what a Jew may or may not eat—all that concerns *kashrut*—are based on the principle that a man cannot live a higher, nobler life of the spirit without having the body undergo some suitable preparation for it. From one point of view, the precepts concerning what is allowed and what is forbidden to eat make up a sort of diet of sanctity, a system of instructions guiding a person's choice of food so that he may derive maximum good from the mutual influence of body and soul. As regards holiness, in the Jewish view the eating of forbidden food is not only a transgression, and so a unification with the domain of evil, but also an act damaging to the network of relations between body and soul. The principle involved here is that food is a matter of levels of essence, graduating in quality of being from the level of matter to that of a living thing, plants, animals, and special kinds of animals, with a proportionately increasing number of restrictions in the way each type of food is prepared and eaten. Thus in the domain of matter nothing is actually prohibited, because this domain is not sensitive to distinctions between the holy and the unholy. Even in the domain of vegetation, the

only restrictions relate to that which grows in the Land of Israel. All that grows outside the Holy Land is considered edible
at all times, whereas rules limit the eating of things grown
within the country, on the premise that the holiness of the land
gives things a higher level of being and a sensitivity to holiness.

The principle is more conspicuous in the domain of life, of
animal meat. There are, of course, several categories of prohibition. First, all living creatures without backbone are absolutely
forbidden. Most fish with fins and scales are permitted, and the
others are not. Also, there is no special preparation needed for
eating fish. Of fowl, there is a certain list of birds that one may
eat; but they have to be slaughtered in a special way, with the
recitation of certain prayers, with the least possible amount of
pain and suffering, with the letting of all the blood, and so
forth, so that the meat may be fit to merge with the human
body. Even more severe are the rules concerning the eating of
the higher animals—only a small number of which are permitted. The slaughtering process and the preparation before cook-
ing are prescribed with exactitude. The mixing of certain types
of foods, like meat and milk products, is absolutely forbidden.

Altogether the mixing of two different orders of things is a
general prohibition in the *Halakhah*, even beyond the dietary
laws of *kashrut*. To be sure, not in every realm of existence do
we know the frontiers of distinction between one order and another, but the Torah has specified a number of them for the
sake of maintaining a degree of purity. The basic principle is, of
course, not purity for its own sake but the need to bring all
things in the world to the state of *Tikkun* or perfection, to raise
them up by correcting, remedying, and setting them right, to

re-create a thing by stripping it to its essential, to redeem it by allowing it to be its utmost. So that the act of eating something should not be a destruction and a ravaging, but a *Tikkun* or consecration of the food. And the eating of impure food or improperly mixed food depresses, and causes a person to descend or diminish in terms of level of being.

Therefore, too, eating and drinking on Sabbaths and festival days becomes more than a satisfying of normal instincts; it is a *mitzvah* in itself. Because on such holy days the nation can better raise up and hallow the things of this world, and the feast becomes an occasion of unity with the Creator. When the Temple stood, ritual sacrifice was itself an occasion for a communal meal in which man participated with the Higher Power in an act of communion. To this day an ordinary table is considered to be a sort of altar at which the one who partakes of food performs an analogous act, however incompletely, elevating matter to the level of man by making it serve human purpose and drawing certain forces away from the world into the active domain of holiness. Extreme care has therefore to be exercised with respect to what is eaten, and the manner in which one eats has to be consistent with the purpose of consecration. Eating is not a casual hedonistic act; it is a ceremony.

A similar attitude prevails on the subject of sexual life. In Judaism, sex is never looked on as something wrong or shameful; it is, on the contrary, considered to be a high level of action potentially capable of bringing out the noblest attributes, not only in the realm of individual feeling, but also in the realm of holiness. And it is nevertheless precisely because of this potential that strict restraints are called for. Indeed, the whole order of relations among the various worlds may be conceived in images of intimate engagement, a kind of sexual contact between one world and another, between one level of being and another. That is why sexual relations themselves have an enormous influence on the soul. All this, besides their primary power—to create a new human being—makes it clear why it is necessary to be extremely respectful to and solicitous about all that concerns the use of the power of sex. In principle, Judaism does not see sexuality only as an instrument for the propagation of the human race, a means of being fruitful and multiplying. The relations between a man and a woman are an organic network, becoming an entity in itself. It brings about the creation of another unity, the family, which is the basic cell of social existence. More profoundly, the family unit is part of the integration of the human individual. In other words, the unattached individual is not yet a whole person; the whole individual is always double, man and woman. Even though each one of a couple is obligated to do his or her own work—physically and spiritually—still the order of their mutuality is what puts each of them on the level of humanity.

Consequently, sexual relations outside the family-creating couple are forbidden. The prohibitions on all other sexual relations are derived from the fact that in essence such relations do not bring about the level of wholeness or unity required of a human being. Although the command "to be fruitful and multiply" is only a part, and not a necessary part, of the intention and meaning of sexual life, it is a matter of principle that the sexual life should be based on relations whose essence comprises the possibility at least of procreation. This principle, in turn, derives from the Jewish view of holiness as something that has such a living reality it must be fertile, capable of growth and development and the bearing of fruit. Similarly, anything that lacks this potential for procreation and growth—whatever has no relation at all to the creation of a new form—is close to the realm of corruption, death, and evil.

The restrictions on the exercise of sexuality are therefore intended mainly to confine it to the family-making unit, to the man-woman, masculine-feminine interaction, and to the wholeness and perfection resulting therefrom, and to the bringing forth of new life accordingly. For the same reason, eroticism is confined to its proper framework. When sexuality and eroticism spread wildly and the life force is expended without any real inner meaning, sex relations become an abysmal process of corruption, in the sense that great divine powers are abused and wasted. The precepts of sexual purity, the regulations concerning sexual habits, and the times for sex within the family are intended to integrate this life cycle with the greater cycles of existence and at the same time to use the power of sex in order to raise one up to a higher level.

One of the central pillars of Jewish thought has always been the *Tikkun* of society, the task of setting it right, of keeping it firmly based on cooperative effort and the harmonious functioning of its individual members. Indeed, there is much more to the Torah than a specific definition of the *mitzvot* and transgressions. Not only is there no total retirement from life, there is general insistence on maintaining a certain vigilance about the welfare of the society and working toward a better world. Hence, too, the overall prohibition against the destruction of

anything that has use and value, and the instruction to be occupied with things that are creative and useful. Concerning society as a whole, every unsocial action, whether specifically
forbidden by Torah, is considered a transgression. A person has
to appear far better to others than he appears to himself; in fact,
the other person has to be like the image of God, and any injury to him is like doing an injury to the divine image in oneself. Following this line of thought, just as physical injury to
one's fellow man is forbidden, so also are lying, theft, guile, and
the like. Offenses like insult, slander, and gossip are in many
ways considered far more severe misdeeds than specifically religious or ritual transgressions. Not for nothing has it been said
that while the Day of Atonement (*Yom Kippur*) provides atonement for transgressions committed by man against God, it does
not provide atonement for transgressions committed against
one's fellow man. Because the latter wrongdoing is doubly sinful, involving an evil to man as well as to God, and so long as
the transgressor does not make amends to his neighbor, he cannot expect a pardon and atonement from God.

Social obligations include all family relations, such as the du-
ties of parents to children and the honor due to parents, and
range from the need to worry about all members of a household
to concern for one's friend and comrade. A recurrent and
deeply entrenched phrase in the tradition is *gemilut hassadim*
("the granting of kindnesses") which denotes a general *mitzvah*
to do good and help people in every way possible, whether in
material things or otherwise. The intention of this *mitzvah* is
that society and its members have to repair the ills of social and
individual misfortune. Which brings one to an essential princi-

ple in Judaism, that of self-respect—a concept that includes and goes beyond personal dignity and the honor of the community. It derives from the fundamental sense of respect for and the love of one's fellow man as expressed in the most simple and formal of human relations and in the requirement to help anyone who slips and falls to regain balance and stand on his own feet. A necessary corollary to this principle is the care taken to avoid giving offense to the dead. This does not mean some cult of the dead. It is rather a direct continuation of the respect given to the person one knew when alive, respect for the body that was once in the divine image.

Thus in all walks of social existence, the obligation is not only to refrain from things that may be injurious to others, but to act deliberately and wholeheartedly to improve and raise the order of life. There is, for instance, the ancient custom of giving a tenth of one's wealth to charity, to help others in any way that seems appropriate. Although the general aim of the ethic is to perfect the society, every individual is related to in supreme earnestness. A single person is reckoned as though he were a world, a totality unto itself, and the concern for him has to be the same mixture of love and respect that one renders to a divine manifestation.

The same kind of approach is valid, of course, for the nation as a whole. The Jewish people should see itself as a single large family, as a special social entity with personal ties kept close and firm. This national entity is considered primary, not as a sum of many separate parts but as that which results when one rises in level from one soul to another and reaches such a greater perfection that all the souls of Israel constitute one general soul which is the divine manifestation in the world. Therefore, the various souls relate to one another as parts of one body; and from this point of view, the higher a person rises, the trials and difficulties involved are increasingly concerned with one's fellow man. For every human being is a part of the single soul that is the spirit of the entire universe.

11

Prayer

Communal and Private Worship

From time to time, a person emerges from the world he inhabits, the world of his life, and addresses God. This is, in essence, the moment of prayer. And from that intimate, essential point, prayer grows and broadens in the form of consciousness, of love, and of words.

Our sages say that prayer is called *"avodah"*—worship. The same word was used to describe the Temple sacrifices. But while the sacrifices entailed physical activity, prayer is the "worship of the *heart*"—as in the verse, "Serve Him with all your heart."

The Temple service had two aspects: the national obligation to offer sacrifices (such as the morning and evening burnt offerings) and the obligation of individuals to bring personal sacrifices (upon making a vow, for example). Prayer shares these two aspects. It is an ongoing obligation of the Jewish people as a whole, and the obligation of each individual as well.

Communal and Personal: Which Takes Precedence?

The Talmud poses a question that it does not, ultimately, re-solve: do the three daily prayer services correspond to the com-munal sacrifices or were they originally instituted by the Patriarchs? This question is not merely historical, but addresses the role and meaning of prayer.

If the prayer service corresponds to the communal sacrifices, then it is not the act of lone individuals gathered together; rather, it is a communal activity in which the individual takes part. Although *halacha* allows for individual expression within the prayer, the community prays as a whole, its individual members serving the communal intent.

But if it is so that the prayer service was established by the Pa-triarchs, then prayer is essentially a personal, individual endeavor, one's self-expression as he turns to God. This is because the Patri-archs (Abraham, Isaac, and Jacob) are not only the ancestors of the Jewish people; more importantly, they represent the three principal modes—love, fear, and compassion—with which the Jewish soul identifies, and through which each Jew prays.

These different points of view are mirrored in the structure of the synagogue. In a synagogue built upon the communal model, the prayers are well organized and punctiliously recited, following authoritative, meticulously preserved traditions of tune and text. Such a synagogue is a representation of the Tem-ple, which a person enters as he would come to the "House of God" (Genesis 28:17), not to express a personal connection but to meld his prayer into that of the community. The architecture of such a synagogue reflects the majesty that was the hallmark of the Temple.

On the other hand, in a synagogue focused on the individual, the work of prayer is one's personal challenge. The congregation may pray in concert—but equally, one person may choose to stride from one end of the room to the other, another may be singing, another wandering about, and yet a fourth sitting in a corner and meditating. This is not prayer as communal experience—not prayer corresponding to the communal sacrifices—but the prayer of the qualities that characterize Abraham, Isaac, and Jacob, as each of us experiences these traits with our human souls and divine sparks. The architecture of these synagogues, such as that of the humble Hasidic *shtiebl,* creates a personal prayer space, shaped primarily in order for the individual to turn to God without distraction or interruption.

In actuality, these two modes are not necessarily that starkly different, and they even overlap. Sometimes a person stands in a congregation but he prays as though alone; at other times, a number of individuals praying by themselves are connected on a soul level, and so create a unified community.

The Institutionalization of Prayer

These two perspectives are the expression of a yet deeper divide: between prayer as defined by the Torah as "worship of the heart" and the structure of prayer as it exists today; between the frameworks constructed by our sages over the course of centuries and the personal frameworks people create for themselves.

In the early generations, every individual prayed according to the urgings of his heart, speaking his own words as best he could and whenever he wished to do so. Only after the destruction of the first Temple, when a certain alienation from Judaism developed—as reflected in the fact that people found it hard to express themselves in prayer—did the members of the Great Assembly formulate the set prayer services.

These services are of a communal nature. The core prayer, the *Shmoneh Esrei*, contains many requests for blessings that not every individual needs at every moment.

There is a request for knowledge and there is a request for sustenance and a request for healing. Sometimes a person needs knowledge, but does not need rain, and sometimes one needs neither rain nor knowledge, but needs health. But because the text of the prayer is general, it contains many requests among them. The individual does not pray only for himself, but also for others and for the community.

In a profounder sense, there is no dividing line between them. The community incorporates the individual, and the totality of the Jewish people is incorporated within each person.

A Fixed Schedule

The fixed structure of prayer—the text, the set times, and the other attendant rules—gives a formal, well-defined way to fulfill the commandment to pray. But beyond that, it helps us to arrive at the inner essence of prayer: turning to God in our hearts.

Sometimes a person's heart spontaneously opens, and he finds himself able to stand before God. But such moments of inspiration are infrequent, indeed so rare that it was deemed necessary to designate specific times for prayer. Without such a schedule, a person might seldom think of God. But because we are bound by fixed prayer times, we are obligated to turn to God three times a day, and thus form some sort of daily relationship with the Almighty. Although this meeting with God may be under duress, it is at least a point of regular contact that does not depend on one's mood, disposition, or inner preparation. It is like setting a date, which depends on finding the time and the place. And when it is set up, one comes.

The Soul's Need for Prayer

Each of us has the need to pray; it is an expression of the soul, which yearns—with or without our conscious recognition—to turn to the holy. In some people, this need is so clear and strong that their problem is not how to find time for prayer but how to constrict prayer within the time allotted to it. Others must rely on the formal prayer schedule in order to pray at all.

We can compare the need to pray with the feeling of hunger—which is a deeper analogy to prayer than may be initially supposed. Although we have an instinctive need to eat, we subject that need to a schedule. Sometimes a person eats not because he is hungry but because mealtime has arrived. So, every individual has an inner need to pray, to pour out his heart in the worship of God. However, that need is not necessarily synchronized with the formal prayer services.

So frequent is the disconnect between need and schedule that it raises challenging questions. Should a person pray only when he is prepared, in the right mood, and undistracted—or is it enough that he conduct himself appropriately? If he cannot keep his mind on the words of prayer, is that no prayer at all—or is it enough that he applies himself as best he can?

Blending the Inner and the Outer

There is no perfect response to these problems. There is the practical answer, which is based on the assumption that in our time people lack the proper concentration in prayer, and so Jewish law demands that we engage in the prayer services even if we are not in the mood.

Alternately, perhaps, one should not care about inner feelings but stick to the external objective element. What if, at the time of prayer, one does not feel prepared, one is anxious, or one is absorbed in other things? If one can somehow control his emotions and at least assume the position of a person standing before a King, does he have an inner feeling of prayer? Is there a real prayer and true intention beyond fulfilling the halachic ruling to pray at set times and in fixed forms?

In contrast, there is the ideal—to blend our inner desires with the communal service. Such a prayer combines a person's outer actions and inner intent, his words and heart. When a person achieves this, the inner movement of his soul is in complete accord with the framework of the prayer service.

Thus, when the Talmudic sage Rabbi Chanina ben Dosa prayed on someone's behalf, he would know that his prayer had been accepted if his words flowed fluently, for then he felt his soul to be aligned with his prayers. But if he felt he was making an effort, as though he were forcing his words against reality, he knew that his prayer had been rejected.

The most complete example of such a prayer is found in the story of Rabbi Chiya and his sons. When Rabbi Chiya recited the words of prayer, "He causes the wind to blow," the wind blew; when he said, "He causes the rain to fall," rain fell. When Rabbi Chiya said, "He brings the dead back to life," the entire world shook.

When a person is connected to his prayer to such a profound extent, he has no need to work at aligning himself with the words of prayer, or with an external framework, simply because that framework is no longer external to him; a total unity exists between his soul, the words that he is reciting, and objective reality.

Such prayer is not "service" in the sense of "work," because it is not an effort to change something within oneself or within reality. Indeed, this is just the joining of the prayer that arises spontaneously from this worldly reality with the words of prayer.

Many people have often had the same experience, when they read or hear something and feel that it is just what they would have wanted to say. So a person praying on this level feels that the words of the prayer book mirror exactly his own thoughts and desires. He himself flows together with the prayer service, ascending and descending from psalm to psalm, from blessing to blessing, from one level of reality to another, moving with the services like a traveler journeying through various vistas. He is on Mt. Moriah, present at Abraham's sacrifice of Isaac; he is then in the Temple, offering sacrifices; he rises and praises God together with the heavens; he stands at the Red Sea as he recites, "Then sang Moses"; he joins the angels in proclaiming God's holiness, rising with the *ophanim* in a thunderous chorus facing the seraphim; he enters into a state of oneness when he recites the *Sh'ma;* he surrenders everything to God when he states "and you shall love"; and he stands before God with complete self-effacement in the *Shmoneh Esrei.*

In such prayer, the person praying and the words being prayed are one; there is no longer a dividing line between one's inner reality and one's outer expression, between communal ritual and the personal voice of the heart.

At times such unity is achieved when people dance to a tune: the tune and dance blend into one. The melody dances and the dance sings; it is impossible to distinguish between them and to say which came first, which inspired the other.

This contrast between formal and inspired prayer may be seen in an apparent contradiction in the Sabbath morning prayer, *Nishmat Kol Chai.* At first, this prayer states that "even if our mouths were filled with song like the sea and our tongues with melody like the multitude of its waves, and our lips with praise like the vistas of the firmament . . . we still could not adequately acknowledge You." So great is God's love, so wonderful are His deeds, that we cannot sufficiently acknowledge them; whatever the mouth can speak is not enough, and we can only remain silent. Yet then, in another section, the prayer states that we *can* express our feelings: "And so the limbs that You have given us and the spirit and soul that You have breathed into our nostrils and the tongue that You have placed in our mouths shall acknowledge, bless, praise and glorify."

When a person has to force himself to sing to God and praise Him, no amount of effort will suffice; but when the tongue speaks by itself, when the mouth and lips sing of their own volition, when he finds himself bowing spontaneously, then he is indeed able to acknowledge and praise God. At that moment, a person and his prayer are not two entities, but one unity. It is not that he recites prayer, for the prayer itself is praying, flowing from the song of his own nature.

The Talmud recounts that King David's harp would play by itself at midnight. And the Jerusalem Talmud comments that in the verse, "When the musician would play music, the hand of God would be upon him," the word for "musician" should be read as "musical instrument" instead: the instrument would play by itself. Why do our sages insist on conflating musician and musical instrument? The answer is that when a person attains the perfect level of prayer, he himself is an instrument playing music spontaneously; he has become the instrument of song, of prophecy, of prayer. The melody is his, and his entire being is none other than an instrument expressing that prayer.

Such self-expression—in which a person links himself not only to an inner state of holiness but also to the external structures of holiness—is prayer on the highest level. Although such an achievement is exceedingly rare, we must make it our goal—we must know that such a level exists. Even if such a state is not common, it can sometimes spark into flame from time to time in a psalm, a blessing, or even a word.

Preparing for Prayer

To reach such a state of sustained prayer is impossible without proper preparation, either before or during the prayer service. In either case, it is known as "the service—or work—of prayer." This work is not one's goal, but a path toward self-transformation and self-rectification that leads one to a true way: to a prayer in which a person's soul expresses the truth of the words he is speaking.

On infrequent occasions, such inspired prayer comes as a state of grace, a gift from heaven. But the true solution is only found through hard work: the struggle of spirit and flesh to bring our soul into alignment with the words that we speak.

Understanding the Words

The first step to every inner intention is to clearly understand the words of the prayer book. Listening to the words one says, on the most basic level, is the foundation for inner listening. Only when one hears the words, can he hear also what lies beyond the words.

The notion of "understanding the words" can be defined on many levels. But it surely contains the simple notion of understanding the plain meaning of the words. This is what separates one who understands a language from one who does not. And when one does not understand the language, he cannot hope that prayer will have an effect on a higher level of intention.

In previous generations, there were people who reached high levels of religious fervor by reciting words from a prayer book that they did not comprehend. A person would hear something, give it a meaning—right or wrong—and have from it a holy enthusiasm. That blend of ignorance and simplicity no longer exists. For better or worse, we have left behind that world of simple faith. We cannot build any deep connection on words that we do not understand.

Those familiar with the prayer book from childhood face an additional challenge. Believing themselves already well versed in prayer, as adults they are unlikely to study its texts. If there was a phrase or passage that they did not understand as children, the chances are great that they will never understand it. And as they repeat these phrases year after year, they do not even realize that they fail to understand them.

Understanding the simple meaning of the words is necessary—but not, however, sufficient. Approaching the words of the prayer book in a cold or academic fashion (focusing on the grammar or on the sources of the various prayers) is not prayer—quite to the contrary. When a person prays, he is standing and speaking to God. If he were speaking warmly to a friend, it would never occur to him to analyze his words as though reviewing a speech or an essay—how much more so when he is speaking directly to the King of the universe.

Extending Our Concentration

Even when a person understands the words and recites them in heartfelt prayer—which is to say, as speech to God—he will likely find it difficult to maintain that focus for an extended period. The prayer service is not brief, and focusing one's thoughts is not at all simple. Indeed, the essence of the work of prayer may be said to be the struggle to maintain one's concentration for the length of the services.

In order to focus successfully on what he is saying, a person must find his words meaningful for him: not something that is entirely incomprehensible, nor something that is so well known that it has lost any meaning. As our sages state, a person's prayer must be new: it must have a fresh perspective and meaning, and not merely repeat yesterday's prayers.

The need to stay focused and attentive raises an age-old question: Is it preferable to pray quickly or slowly? On the one hand, maintaining one's focus for a lengthy period of time is difficult, and so when one prays quickly there is less opportunity for irrelevant thoughts to arise. On the other hand, if one prays too quickly, one may lack the time he needs to reach a state of focused attention.

This dilemma has no single answer. For those who are able to reach a state of concentration but unable to maintain it for long, quick prayer is preferable; others need more time to reach a true feeling of connection to God. And every individual changes: sometimes he cannot pray slowly, and at other times he can. To adhere to a rigid regimen would only cause him to lose the opportunity of inspired prayer.

Self-Delusion

There is another and deeper problem: that of self-delusion. Just as people sometimes delude themselves that they are "in love," so can they believe that they are praying, that they are having a religious experience, even though it is only a false spirituality. A person may think he is in communion with holiness, in a state of divine love or fear—yet he is experiencing no more than illusions: not an experience coming from a true inner soul connection, but from an almost physiological phenomenon. A person finds himself in a certain atmosphere, in the company of others who enhance that mood; he is exposed to music or scents, and he responds. By way of analogy, sometimes when one person yawns, everyone else follows suit—not because they are tired, but simply as an imitative mechanism.

The same can occur in prayer: a person wraps himself in a prayer shawl and sways back and forth, and he imagines that he is religiously moved; the focus and tension caused by the atmosphere, by the fact that he is standing and reciting words of prayer, appear to him to be a meaningful experience. He may sing as he prays and believe that he has been swept up in the love of God—but in truth this might be merely an external movement—a prayer tune but not a prayer.

This is a serious concern. A person who is sincerely attempting to find his way to his inner being should indeed make use of external means to reach a state of concentrated attention. But since those means may arouse counterfeit emotions, how can he know if his intense feelings of prayer are true or delusory? The answer is that "the lip of truth will be established forever" (Proverbs 12:19). Something that is true lasts; truth has permanence, and falsehood is transitory.

A false prayer experience may be compared to the phenomenon known as false pregnancy. A woman shows all the signs of pregnancy, from morning sickness to an extended belly to birth pangs; but in the end there is nothing—only the illusion of pregnancy. The proof of authenticity is whether something has been brought into the world. If there is nothing but air, then there was nothing but air from the very beginning.

If after religious rapture passes, nothing remains, the absence of emotion indicates that all along it was no more than the imitation of true feeling. The value of a person's prayer lies not in how much he cried out, how much he swayed, nor even how strong his emotions were, but in what remains of his experience after the prayers are over.

The rebbe of Kotzk commented on the blessing in the prayer book, *yishtabach*, as follows. The prayer states that God "chooses musical songs." The word for "musical"—*shirei*—can be related to *shirayim*—meaning, "remains." God chooses not "songs" but what remains after that song is over. If the song is true, it does not fade; if the feeling is genuine, it will leave a resonance. These "remains" are not necessarily something intellectual or even emotional; they are merely an impression of something that had been. And the indication of whether the experience left such an impression is whether some change has been wrought in the individual. If the answer is yes, that is all the proof that is needed to show that this was indeed a genuine experience.

It is important to distinguish between truth and delusion in prayer not only because it would be a shame to misrepresent ourselves to God (or to deceive ourselves), but because it is dangerous. There is a law in economics that bad pennies drive out the good ones. So it is in spiritual life. False experiences drive out true feelings. When a person is filled with illusory sensations, he loses the ability to identify a genuine sensation. Had he experienced no emotions whatsoever, he would have at least have been aware of that; but if he falsely imagines that he is experiencing feeling or that he is genuinely praying, then he no longer has the chance to attain true emotion. And so in order to allow himself to experience an authentic sensation, he must actively work to give up any false emotions that he has.

The Necessity of Concentration

The "work of prayer," in brief, consists of being in tune, paying progressively deeper attention to what one is saying until one's heart is in tune with one's words. This inner work precedes prayer itself. Like the foundation of a building, it is the basis of one's concentration—whether it is the mystical unifications of the Ari or "praying like this little child." There is a world of difference between focused attention based on kabbalistic secrets, in which the words of prayer are understood on a profound plane, and simple prayer, which focuses on the literal meaning of the words. But they both possess the same necessary foundation: attention to what one is saying. If a person recites a prayer that is not his—if he is merely speaking someone else's words—that is not truly prayer. A person should mean truly what he says; on whatever level he speaks, it should be the reality in which he lives and prays. The main point of prayer is that "*I* am praying." When *I* am saying my own prayer, then it is on a very high level.

How can we pray with genuine understanding and feeling? How can we engage in the worship of the heart that prepares our soul to pray? There is no certain formula, no guaranteed mechanism. However, there are methods that can at least point us in the proper direction. Here we shall discuss three.

First Method: Wrestling with the Prayer Book

The first, simplest, and perhaps most natural technique has been suggested by a certain sage: One should pray, he said, in the same way that one quarrels. One says a word, the other says a word, until things get heated. This approach does not require preparation before prayer; one simply takes the prayer book and struggles with it on all the points that we have discussed: understanding the words, concentration, and consciousness in relation to and about truth. One toils over every line of text, every word, every part of a word, attempting to squeeze some meaningful kernel out of it. In addition, one struggles over the question, "Am I merely repeating the words of others, or is this something of particular relevance to me?"

The success of this method depends on consistency, extended focus, and effort. This is quite difficult to achieve, particularly since the prayer service does not have a homogenous texture: it has passages in which we throw ourselves on God's mercy, remember His miracles and thank Him, experience elevated joy, and engage in humble self-reflection. Each of these is a different stratum of feeling, a different chain of internal experiences. It is hard enough to enter into a sustained mood—how much more difficult to accompany the words of the prayer book, ascending and descending as they do, so that—for instance—we recite the *Shmoneh Esrei* with the consciousness of standing directly before God with no intermediary, then immediately afterward, in the *Nefilat Apayim*, we descend radically from divinity into created reality. This is the nature of the entire prayer service: it moves from one extreme to the other, ascending and descending—which makes extremely difficult demands on a person's psyche.

A person's thoughts tend to be random and easily distracted, and can quickly shift from the holy to the profane. We must work hard to keep our minds focused; we must struggle with all our might. This battle to maintain proper concentration has no clear ending. If a person's only goal were to recite the words as written, he could succeed within a certain amount of time; but struggling with the prayer experience, plumbing the meaning of word after word and sentence after sentence, is a never-ending process. Sometimes a person may apply himself fruitlessly—even if he applies himself repeatedly, his efforts may be in vain. Our tradition refers to prayer as a time of battle; in this battle, as in any other, one may lose.

Nevertheless, even when one has gained nothing, if one determines that next time one will pray with intensity, if one expresses that commitment repeatedly and believes that such a goal is attainable, then it truly is within one's reach. When a person determinedly focuses on the words of prayer, he may be sure that one day something within him will burst into flame. Even if he must repeat some passage in the prayer book a thousand times, he will reach the point where the words resonate with him and he recites them as an expression of his own feelings.

This method of serving God was taught by the Baal Shem Tov, and he illustrated it with a homiletic reading of God's command to Noah: "Make a shining stone for the ark." The word "ark" in Hebrew—*teivah*—can also mean "word." A person must work on a word of prayer even when it is like a lifeless stone, until it begins to gleam and becomes like a glass through which divinity shines. And how does one do so? The verse continues: "Come, you and your entire household, into the *teivah*"; a person comes and puts all of his being—his thoughts and feelings, his memories and dreams—into a word of prayer, its denotation and connotation. Thus does he proceed, word after word and sentence after sentence.

This approach to the service of prayer does not require any particular preparation: one simply takes the prayer book and struggles with one's awareness, with one's concentration, working hard so that as one prays something will occur, the barrier between oneself and the prayer book will dissolve until, one day, as one pronounces one word, the prayer book will cease to be a text from which one is reciting and turn into a book in which one's own self is written.

Second Method: Study

The next approach also requires that a person intellectually plumb the depths of his prayer's meaning. But in this case one's efforts are planned, based on a preparatory learning session.

This session of learning does not necessarily involve the prayer book text; it must, however, be concerned with awareness of the divine. The purpose of this learning is not merely intellectual acquisition but study that is directed intentionally toward the work of prayer, to penetrate all aspects of one's psyche, and to enhance one's prayer experience. This learning is an emotional endeavor that involves one's full concentration and emotional commitment.

The purpose of this study is to incorporate it into prayer. The more in-depth a person's study and the more details he contemplates, the more he can transform that topic into a real and tangible image, as though it is standing before his eyes. When he begins to pray, his every word and sentence is spoken within the context of his relationship with that image. He prays within the concept; he develops it and derives meaning from it throughout the prayer service; he seeks its echo on every page and in every word. The prayer experience, with all of its variations, with its ascents and descents, becomes the expression of the thought that he has so profoundly studied.

For instance, a person can meditate on the meaning of gratitude. He begins from the simplest notion: acknowledging the good that another has done. He then considers in-depth questions such as, "What is appreciation composed of? What is the nature of its being? How does it connect us to God?" Having delved into these questions from every angle, he brings the topic to his prayers. He searches for the themes of appreciation and gratefulness in the words that he is reciting—in his praise, requests, supplication, and thanks. All of these now reflect appreciation, until he reaches the *modim derabbanan*: "We thank You . . . for that we thank You." The foundation stone and précis of all prayer is to thank God for the gift of being able to pray.

Such depth of concentration does not mean that one must interpret every word anew, but that one tries repeatedly to see the inner meaning that formed within every sentence of prayer.

There is no need to change any word, nor its meaning; one must only understand its implications as if for the first time. That type of study takes hold of him and electrifies him, as it draws into itself all the words of prayer and gives them new meaning.

This experience is not a rare phenomenon; to the contrary, we constantly experience its equivalent in other areas of our lives. When a person desires something passionately, when he has a memory of an experience or a strong emotion, he will find it everywhere and in everything—while working or being at home, walking in the street or meeting people—anything will cause him to awaken the emotion, directly or indirectly, as a similarity or as a contrast. For instance, if a person's close relative is ill, then he relates every blessing, every request, every psalm in the prayer service to that; he is not able to understand the words of prayer in any other way.

A metaphor for this kind of prayer is song. The Hebrew word for song, *shir*, can also mean "circle." These two meanings are intertwined. Every song is, in some way, a circular path, always turning back to its refrain. After each new stanza, that refrain yields a new depth and meaning. The same applies to prayer: one takes a topic and "sings" it, one returns to the refrain, one looks for it in the word and prayer until that topic crystallizes, becomes one strand of experience, an experience that one reinforces as one proceeds, making it ever more clear, warmer, and emotionally fulfilling.

When one meditates on a thought for a sustained period of time, beyond the moment in which it arose in one's mind, it becomes tangible and real. That passing idea then becomes a meaningful thought that can build a complete structure. Concentration and memory are like a song repeating its refrain within the words of prayer. If a person has a fleeting thought of love or fear of God, and he takes that thought and sings it, repeats it again and again until he makes it a rhapsody, a tapestry, then he has turned an initial spark into a fervent flame.

The power in this way of prayer lies in continuity. We engage in the work of prayer by taking a topic and working on it—not at random, not by happenstance, but together with the prayer—guiding the prayer in a specific direction over a period of time, whether that be an hour, a week, or a month. Within that time frame and within those words of prayer, this topic is woven into the words of prayer, and it not only touches but is carved into one's soul. Slowly, as truth is carved free of illusion—that which is permanent is carved from that which is transitory—one no longer has simply a single point of emotion and fervor, but a line that leads one from one rung to the next on the ladder of prayer.

Third Method: To Set Aside an Hour

We find the third approach to meaningful prayer described in the *mishnah:* "The early Hasidim would set aside an hour and then pray, so that they would turn their hearts to God."

This path is of an extremely individual nature. Here, a person comes to terms with the truth of himself; he attempts to reach, within himself, the ideal of perfection. Since it is very difficult—indeed, almost impossible—to explain and describe such a thing to another, this path is shrouded in mystery; it is a path upon which few proceed.

Like the previous approach, this one is based on preparation before prayer; however, this preparation is not accomplished by studying or meditating upon some topic, but by aligning one's mind and heart, of clarifying one's personal experience, of extracting truth as it pertains to oneself.

R. Leibele Eiger asked the Kotzker rebbe what to tell his noted grandfather, R. Akiva Eiger, when the latter would question the Hasidic custom of delaying one's prayers. The rebbe replied that this is a *halachah* to be found in Maimonides' writings. If a worker is hired to chop down trees and he spends most of the day sharpening his axe, he gets paid in full. It is possible to chop down trees with a dull axe—or, for that matter, with a piece of flint—but the work will require tremendous effort, will take a great deal of time, and the outcome will be unsatisfactory. But when the tool is sharpened, the work can be completed quickly. This way of preparation for prayer is the same: a person directs himself, sharpens his sense of the presence of God so that it becomes real, and only then does he pray.

In the first two approaches, the service and the effort take place during the prayer itself. But in this case, we may say that all of the work—besides the prayer service itself—is incorporated into the preparation. All of the work of directing and focusing oneself have already reached full expression before the prayer service has begun, and so during the prayer service there is no need to pray at length; from the pinnacle of truth a person has already attained, his prayer streams spontaneously.

The difficulty in this approach is in preparing the "tool." One does not study a topic or the framework of a specific prayer service but directs oneself to become an instrument of service. The demands of this path are greater than that of other modes of prayer. The issue with which a person must contend is not an intermediary step—such as understanding, focus, or preparation—but the point of truth itself. The question one must face before praying is whether one is able and willing to stand in the presence of God. The purpose of this preparation is to bring a person to the conclusion that he truly wishes, and truly can, pray at this moment. This may take one half hour, three hours, or ten hours. Everything is predicated on the condition that he will not begin to pray until he is truly ready to do so, no matter how long that may take.

The story in the Talmud about Choni the Circle-Maker is instructive. Choni did not make requests of God as others did, for he brooked no denial of his prayers. At a time of drought, he drew a circle, stepped into it, and declared that he would not leave that circle until rain fell—and God sent down the rain. The Bible tells a similar story about Jabez (Chronicles I 4:10), who made a request of God on the condition that "if You do not fulfill my request, I will descend to Sheol!" Immediately, "God brought about what he requested." Apparently, a person has permission to turn to God with utter stubbornness, truly feeling that he would rather die than accept failure, and then God will give him everything.

The Service of the Heart

All approaches to prayer are difficult, demanding, and wondrous. They are *difficult* because prayer is service, or work; they are *demanding* because prayer corresponds to the sacrifices; and they are *wondrous* because before a person prays he cannot imagine that he will in truth be able to do so.

The Bible speaks of the Levite family of Kehat as "all who come together," and of its related clan, Gershon, as "all who come to gather together." In Aramaic, the word used for "together," *tzava,* means "desire" or "will." Thus, we can homiletically translate these verses as saying that Kehat "has a desire," whereas Gershon only "desires to have a desire." Some people of rare quality possess an internal desire that drives their actions. Others do not yet have that desire—they do, however, desire to have that desire.

And so is it in the way of prayer: one person prays, and another prays that he will be able to pray; one person serves, and another serves so that one day he will truly become a servant of God in the service of the heart, which is prayer.

12

An Additional Note on the *Kiddush* Ritual

THE EVE OF THE SABBATH does not only usher in the day of rest; it has its own particular aspect and significance. Every hour of the preceding afternoon marks another level of an emotionally peaked transition from the six working days of the week to the Sabbath day. The evening before the holy day is therefore itself a climax and a final stage of the transition, to all that the day means, both as a conclusion of the week and as a higher level of existence, beyond the six days of action, beyond time.

This higher level of the Sabbath is bound up with the divine manifestation in the *Sefirah* of *Malkhut* ("kingdom"), which represents the *Shekhinah* and also the totality, the receptacle that absorbs all that occurs, and is also connected with the first *Sefirah*, the Crown. Therefore the quality of Sabbath Eve, which is the summing up of work and events in time, can also be a preparation for the manifestation of the Sabbath as the crown and beginning of time. The *Sefirah* of *Malkhut*, or the *Shekhinah*, represents the divine power as manifested in reality, operating in an infinite variety of ways and means. It has seventy names, each expressing another aspect, another face of this all inclusive *Sefirah*. For *Malkhut* is the seventh of the lower *Sefirot* and, as the last, also includes in itself the entire ten; in other words, it expresses all of the *Sefirot*, each in seven different forms; so that seventy is the key number to the unfolding of the ritual of the evening devoted to *Malkhut* and to the *Shekhinah* which *Malkhut* represents.

What is equivalent in all the manifestations of the *Shekhinah* is that each represents a certain aspect of the feminine. Consequently the symbols and the contents of Sabbath Eve are always oriented to the female, with emphasis on the woman in her universal aspect as well as in terms of the Jewish family.

On entering a home on the eve of the Sabbath, one may see how a dwelling is made into a sanctuary. The table on which are set the white loaves of Sabbath bread and the burning candles recall the Holy Temple with its menorah and its shew bread. The table itself is, as always, a reminder of the altar in the Temple, for eating could and should become an act of sacrifice. In other words, the relation between man and the food he consumes, as expressed in the intention behind the eating of the food, corresponds to the cosmic connection between the material and the spiritual as expressed by every sacrifice on an altar. Especially is this true on the Sabbath, when the Sabbath feast takes on the character of a sacramental act, a sort of communion, in the performance of the *mitzvah* of union of the soul, the body, the food, and the essence of holiness. Therefore at mealtimes the table always has on it a salt container, just as salt had to be on the holy altar as a sign of the covenant of salt. The candles lit by the woman of the house emphasize the light of the

Sabbath, the sanctification of the day, and the special task of the woman as representative of *Shekhinah* of *Malkhut*. There are two loaves of special white bread, called *challah* (some houses have twelve *challot*), covered with a cloth; these also recall the bread from heaven, the manna, which on the Sabbath day came down in double portions covered with a layer of dew.

As part of the preparations for the *Kiddush* ("consecration") ceremony, the members of the household sing or recite the song of praise for the "woman of valor" (Proverbs 31:10–31). The song, with its appreciation for the woman, the mother, the housekeeper, has on this Sabbath Eve a double connotation, as praise for the lady of the house and as glorification of the *Shekhinah* of *Malkhut* who is, in a sense, the mother, the house-keeper of the real world. Following this is the Twenty-third Psalm, expressing the calm trust in God. And one is ready for the *Kiddush* ceremony itself.

In terms of *Halakhah*, the *Kiddush* is the carrying out of the fourth of the Ten Commandments: "Remember the Sabbath Day to keep it holy." At the very beginning of the Sabbath there has to be some act of separation, of consecration, empha-sizing the difference between the work days of the week and the holy day and enabling the soul to move into a state of in-ner tranquility and spiritual receptiveness. To be sure, the words of the consecration are also said at the time of evening prayer and on other occasions; but in Judaism there is a gen-eral principle that, to as great an extent as possible, abstract events or processes and all that pertains to them are bound up with specifics and definite actions. Thus the *Kiddush* consecra-tion is connected with the drinking of wine, which, in turn, becomes part of a ceremony and, in turn, is associated with the Sabbath wine sacrifices of the Holy Temple.

The *Kiddush* cup symbolizes the vessel through which, and into which, the blessing comes. The numerical weight of the letters in the word for drinking cup (*kos*) is the same as that of the letters in that name of God expressing the divine revelation in the world, in nature, in law. And into the cup is poured the bounty, the wine that represents the power of the blessing of the word "wine," whose numerical equivalent is seventy, which is also the number of Sabbath Eve. Wine then evokes the bounty, the great plentitude and power; and red wine especially expresses a certain aspect of the *Sefirah* of *Gevurah*, which also has an aspect of severity and justice. Thus after one has poured most of the wine into the cup, a little water, symbol of grace and love, is added to create the right mixture, or harmony, between *Hesed* and *Gevurah*. After the filling of the cup, which is now the vessel of consecration containing the divine plenty, one places it on the palm of the right hand in such a way that the cup, supported by the upturned fingers, resembles or recalls a rose of five petals. For one of the symbols of *Malkhut* is the rose. And the cup of wine, thus expressing also the *Shekhinah*, stands in the center of the palm and is held by the petal fingers of the rose. The time has come for the recitation of the *Kiddush* prayer itself.

The *Kiddush* is composed of two parts. It begins with that part of the Torah (Genesis 2:1–3) where the Sabbath is first mentioned, and then proceeds to the second half which is a prayer composed by the sages especially for the *Kiddush* and in which the various meanings of the Sabbath are poetically and precisely stated. Between the two parts there is the blessing of the vine, or fruit of the grape. In each of these two parts there are exactly thirty-five words, together making seventy, the number of the Eve of the Sabbath. Before reciting the first words from the Torah, two words are added—the last words of the preceding verse: "the sixth day"—because they fit in with the recitation, "Thus the heavens and the earth were finished . . ." and because the first letters of these words form the abbreviation of the Holy Name. In this first section the Sabbath is treated as the day of the summation and cessation of Creation, as God's day of rest.

The second section, selected and determined by the sages, expresses the other side of the Sabbath, the imitation of God by Israel. Before the blessing of the wine, there are the two words in Aramaic telling those present to get ready for the blessing. The following words of the *Kiddush* express the primary elements of the Sabbath and the special relation between Sabbath and the nation. There is first the declaration "Blessed Art Thou . . . by whose commandments we are sanctified," which is to say that the *mitzvah* is a way of reaching a level of holiness, a way to God. After this the prayer speaks of the chosenness of Israel, as a consequence of which Israel, more than all other nations, has to assume the task of carrying on the act of Creation and its aftermath of rest and holiness. Mention is then made of the exodus from Egypt, as in the version of the Ten Commandments in Deuteronomy (5:15), where the Sabbath, proclaimed as the day of rest from work, recollects the time of slavery in Egypt and likens the Sabbath to the divine act of release from bondage and the bestowal of salvation. So that Sabbath is also the weekly day of freedom, celebrating the release and the exodus from Egypt, as well as the concept of salvation which, as the ultimate in time, is the Sabbath of the world.

And out of this emphasis on divine choice and love and out of the need to understand man's obligation to God to continue and to create and to be able to rise above and beyond creation unto the Sabbath rest, the *Kiddush* prayer concludes with the relation of the Jewish people to the Sabbath and thus closes the circle of the relation between God and man. After the recital of the *Kiddush* the one who has performed the ceremony himself drinks from the cup, thereby participating in that communion of the physical with the spiritual which is the essence of all ritual. And from the same cup drink all those gathered at the table. In this way everyone participates in the meaningful act of introducing the Sabbath, represented by the flowering of the rose, which is the cup of redemption of the individual and of the nation and of the world as a whole.

13

Patach Eliyahu—Elijah Began

THE *TIKKUNEI ZOHAR* opens with two introductions. The second of these describes a convocation of sages (both living and dead), of whom one, Elijah the Prophet, is invited to deliver the opening address.

His statement, a brief description of the basic principles of kabbalah, has become a classic text, recited by many as part of the daily or weekly prayer services, and known by its opening words: *Patach Eliyahu*—"Elijah began."

The Text

> *Elijah opened and said:*
> *Master of the worlds,*
> *You are One*
> *But not in counting.*
>
> *You are exalted beyond all exalted,*
> *More hidden than all hidden;*
> *No thought grasps You at all.*

You are He Who brought forth ten rectifications,
Which we call the ten sefirot,
With which to guide
Concealed worlds that are not revealed
And revealed worlds.

In them You concealed yourself from human beings.
You are He Who ties them and unites them.
Because You are within them,
Whoever separates one
Of these ten sefirot *from the others*
Is considered to have caused a separation within You.

These ten sefirot *proceed in order:*
One long, one short and one intermediate.
You guide them
And no one guides You—
Neither above, nor below, nor from any side.

You prepared garments for them.
From these come the souls of human beings.

You prepared a number of bodies—
which are called bodies
in comparison to the garments covering them.
And they are called in this chapter:
Chesed *(lovingkindness)—the right arm;*
Gevurah *(might)—the left arm;*
Tiferet *(harmony)—the torso.*

Netzach *and* hod *(victory and glory)—the two legs.*
And yesod *(foundation)—the end of the torso,*
The sign of the holy covenant.
Malchut *(kingship) is the mouth.*
It is called the oral Torah.
Chochmah *(wisdom)—that is inner thought,*
Binah *(understanding)—that is the heart;*
With it, the heart understands.
About these [Chochmah and Binah] two it is written:
"The hidden things are for the Lord our God"
(Deuteronomy 29:28).
Keter elyon *(supreme crown)—that is* keter malchut,
the crown of royalty,
Of which the verse states:
"From the very beginning, He tells the end" (Isaiah 46:10).
It is the cranium of tefillin.

Within is the name MaH,
Which is the path of atzilut.

This irrigates the tree
With its limbs and its branches,
Like water irrigating a tree,
Which grows because of that irrigation.

Master of the worlds,
You are the Reason of reasons,
And the Cause of causes.
You irrigate the tree with that flow.

That flow is like a soul to the body,
Giving the body life.

In You, there is no image or likeness
Of anything,
Inside or outside.

You created heaven and earth,
And You brought forth from them
Sun, moon, stars and constellations,
And upon the earth,
Trees, the Garden of Eden, grasses, wild animals, beasts, birds, fish
and human beings.
To know through them of the supreme beings
And how the upper and lower beings function,
And how the lower beings gain awareness of the higher beings.
But no one knows You at all,

And besides You,
There is no Oneness,
Above and below.
You are known as
The Cause of all
And the Master over all.

Each sefirah *has a known name,*
By which the angels are called.
But You have no known name,
For You fill all names.
And You are the wholeness of all.

When You leave them,
All of the names remain
Like a body without a soul.

You are wise,
But not with a known wisdom.
You are understanding,
But not with a known understanding.
You have no known place,
But in order to make Your power and might
known to human beings
And to show them how the world is guided
With judgment and compassion,
For there exist justice and lawfulness
In accordance with the deeds of human beings.
Judgment corresponds to [the sefirah*] of* gevurah.
Lawfulness corresponds to the middle column.
Exacting justice corresponds to holy malchut,
The just scales (Leviticus 19:36),
Two pillars of truth.
A just measure (Leviticus 19:36)—
that is the sign of the holy covenant.

All of this to demonstrate how the world functions,
But not that You have a known [trait of]
exacting justice, which is judgment,
Nor a known lawfulness, which is [associated with] compassion,
Nor any of these measures whatsoever.

"Blessed be God forever, amen and amen" (Psalms 89:63).

Commentary

Elijah opened and said:

The words of Elijah, which begin this supreme session, are not a philosophical description of the worlds above us, but a paean to God. He begins by addressing God as:

Master.

This term has many meanings: Creator, Maker, Ruler, and so forth.

God, states Elijah, is not just the Master of one level of reality, but

Of the worlds—

Multiple levels of reality.

You are—

Elijah addresses God Himself to say that He is higher than and totally other than the ten *sefirot*, the media through which He expresses His will.

One but not in counting.

God is One. We know the number one in mathematics ("counting"). The mathematical here stresses the point that the Divine "One" is not like the mathematical one. In mathematics, the concept of "one" allows for the possibility of an additional one; by the same token, "one" can be divided into parts, into fractions. But when we say that the Divine is One, we are speaking in altogether different terms. There can be no additional "one" to God, for He is unique—"there is no other than He" (Deuteronomy 4:35). Not only does His Oneness deny the existence of any similar being, but in the deepest sense it denies that *anything* exists but that Oneness. Finally, unlike the mathematical one, which can be divided, God's Oneness is indivisible and radically simple.

You are exalted beyond all exalted.

Even reaching higher, to higher and more distant levels, You remain forever beyond all.

More hidden than all hidden.

There exist spiritual worlds that are completely hidden from us, and impenetrable, infinitely beyond our comprehension. You are concealed and hidden even from those realms.

No thought grasps You at all.

The language here is very exact; it does not say that our thinking does not grasp this. No thought whatsoever—of any level, whether that of a human being or even of an entity that is vastly superior to the human mind—can understand God. God transcends all minds. The Divine is not some "Superior mind" but beyond any level of intellect. Intellect, at any level and any power, is not the vessel that can grasp divinity, which is infinite, which is beyond any definition.

You are He Who brought forth—

This phrase implies the emergence into being of something that had once been concealed (as opposed to creation *ex nihilo*): the *sefirot*. This phrase also implies that all these *sefirot* are external to God and not a part of God's essential Being.

Ten rectifications.

That is to say, ten entities that are rectified—this term will be explained (at least in part) further on.

Which we call the ten sefirot.

So they are called in all kabbalistic literature. The greatest of our sages have offered many explanations of this word.

Some explain that the word comes from *sapir*, a diamond. Without a color of its own, it reflects and refracts light or shines with an internal glow.

Others relate it to the word *sipur*, a narrative. The *sefirot* reveal God to His creatures—"the heavens tell the glory of God" (Psalms 19:2). Alternatively, it is because we have permission to speak about the *sefirot* and the levels below them, but not about the levels that transcend them.

Some relate the word *sefirah* to *s'far*, or boundary, for they lie on the border between the infinite and the finite.

Others explain the word as being related to *mispar*, number, for the *sefirot* are defined by their number—that is, ten *sefirot* comprise one basic unit, and the *sefirot* bear a mathematical relationship to each other.

Other explanations are offered as well. All of them enrich the others, although they are not all based on one shared meaning.

With which to guide—

The principal function of the *sefirot* is to guide all the worlds. The *sefirot* are not the revelation of God's inner reality, like words or symbols that reveal the soul or its ideas, but a means of shaping and guiding existence.

They are the equivalent of a tool like an axe, which reveals nothing of the character of the person who wields it. This tool serves his will and acts only by the power of its owner.

Concealed worlds that are not revealed.

These belong to a reality that existed even before our world was created, that are like pre-creation worlds, a reality that is completely hidden—something that "no eye has seen" (Isaiah 64:3).

And revealed worlds.

These are the worlds from the realm of *atzilut* and downward. Although they are not revealed to everyone, they are linked to one another by a chain of causality to our level, and we may know something of them. Therefore, they are considered to be revealed.

In them You concealed Yourself from human beings.

The *sefirot* are supreme instruments through which God reveals Himself to His world and through which He acts upon and activates everything within all the worlds.

But although God is revealed through the *sefirot*, He is equally concealed within them. The divine revelation, whatever form it may take, is never a revelation of God's essence. Rather, it is always mediated by the *sefirot*, which are the instruments of divine self-expression and manifestation. In classical kabbalistic terminology, they are "garments" that both reveal and hide God's essence.

You are He Who ties them.

As shall be explained shortly, each *sefirah* has its own character and therefore each stands beside the other and sometimes against the other. Only You tie them all together so that they act in unison, with one shared goal.

And unites them.

The ten *sefirot* comprise one unit, a complete structure, comparable to the human form with all its limbs. They are a mechanism that God uses to reveal Himself to the worlds that He created.

The *sefirot* have no real existence of their own. We may think of them as ten facets of an object. A facet is a mathematical abstraction. However, when a facet marks the side of a structure, it gains reality. The ten *sefirot* mark the ten "facets" of a divine decagon, as it were. And each angle of this decagon possesses its own individual character.

Only God, Himself, connects the *sefirot* into an integrated unit that incorporates and comprises the divine light, manifesting a different character at each of these ten "points."

Because You are within them—

It is not just that the *sefirot* are ten sides of one essence. But we must remember that this one entity, which unites and ties the *sefirot* together, is You. Therefore,

Whoever separates one of these ten sefirot *from the others—*

And attributes to one *sefirah* special value, believing it to be the most perfect or significant expression of divine revelation, rather than relating it to the sum of the ten *sefirot* as one unit,

Is considered to have caused a separation within You.

From our point of view, these ten *sefirot* constitute the paths along which the divine is revealed. If a person emphasizes one *sefirah* and relates to it as though it is an independent entity, he creates—whether knowingly or not—an idol. At its root, idolatry relates to a partial revelation of the divine as a separate identity.

In its more sophisticated forms, idolatry recognizes the existence of an ultimate power (a God of gods); however, it attributes essence and independent being to a particular representation of the divine. Therefore, the *Zohar* here cautions us not to separate any of the *sefirot* from the divine Being. We are not to view them as individual entities but as one totality, the means of revelation of the one divine Essence.

These ten sefirot *proceed in order.*

Seen from one perspective, the *sefirot* descend in a straight line from *keter* to *malchut.* In that configuration, the *sefirot* have a simple interrelationship of higher and lower, superior and inferior.

However, from another point of view, the *sefirot* form a more spatial structure, in which they are arranged in three vertical columns, forms that have a dimension of breadth in addition to that of length. Each column possesses its own nature. Relationships exist among the *sefirot* that are in vertical order and between the *sefirot* that are next to one another.

In this arrangement, the *sefirot* are arranged in three inverted triangles (see illustration). The first consists of *chochmah* (upper right point), *binah* (upper left point), and *daat* (inverted apex—*daat* is a lower manifestation of *keter*); below that, the second triad consists of *chesed, gevurah,* and *tiferet*; below that is the third triad, consisting of *netzach, hod,* and *yesod.* Below all of these is the tenth *sefirah, malchut.*

The two horizontal points of the triangle are opposing energies that are reconciled by the one below. The initial *sefirah* of

KETER
Primary Will
supreme crown

BINAH
Understanding
heart

CHOCHMA
Wisdom
inner thought

DAAT
Knowledge.
Intelligent
Will
lower brain

Cognition

GEVURAH
Might
left arm

CHESED
Loving-
Kindness
right arm

TIFERET
Harmony
torso

HOD
Glory
left leg

NETZACH
Victory
right leg

YESOD
Foundation
end of torso

Emotion

MALCHUT
Kingship
mouth

Left Line   Middle Line   Right Line

each triad, the upper right-hand point, is a creative, giving force, acting from within; the second *sefirah*, the upper left-hand point of the triad, absorbs and limits what it receives; the third *sefirah*, the lowest point, combines them, incorporating the energies of the two and thus creating a new quality—generally, more perfect or stronger than each of the two previous *sefirot*. This may be understood as an expression of the dialectic of thesis, antithesis, and synthesis.

One long.

This is the right-hand column, consisting of the *sefirot* of *chochmah*, *chesed*, and *netzach*, whose shared characteristics are lovingkindness and patience (in the Hebrew idiom, "long").

One short.

This is the left-hand column, consisting of the *sefirot* of *binah*, *gevurah*, and *hod*, which are characterized by strict justice, and called "short." It is their nature to constrict and conceal the flow of divine energies.

And one intermediate.

This is the middle column, incorporating the *sefirot* of *daat*, *tiferet*, and *yesod*. This central column is a synthesis of the outer columns at either side. It is characterized by compassion, and its influence is paramount.

You guide them.

Even though every *sefirah* has its own nature and characteristics, it does not act independently. You guide and act through the structure of the *sefirot*.

And no one guides You.

Nor influences Your deeds,

Neither above.

In the upper worlds,

Nor below.

In those worlds accessible to us,

Nor from any side.

Whether from holiness or otherwise.

The flow of God's energy acts, but is not acted upon. Nothing that happens in the world, whether for good or for evil, can touch His essence, nor cause any change in Him. As the verse states, "If you sin, what effect do you have on Him?.. . . If you are righteous, what have you given Him?" (Job 35:6–8). Not even the creation of the world caused any change in God—"I God have not changed" (Malachi 3:6).

You prepared garments for them—

For the *sefirot*. The *sefirot* have ways of making themselves known and expressing their essence. These are called their "garments"—just as a person's garments are the way he is revealed. Similarly, a person's words can be considered the "garments" of his thought.

From these come the souls of human beings.

Although the garments of the *sefirot* do not constitute their essence, they are, in themselves, very powerful, and human souls derive from them.

These souls are formed by the combinations (or "unifications") formed by various *sefirot*. The basic elements that create an individual are illuminations that come from various *sefirot*. Every soul is born of a unique combination of the light of the *sefirot*. Just as a sentence is made of individual words, so a person's soul is a unique combination formed by a mingling of the *sefirot*. Souls are not actual fragments of the *sefirot* themselves; rather, they flow from the *sefirot*'s self-expression—their "garments."

You prepared a number of bodies—

For the *sefirot*.

*Which are called bodies in comparison to the
garments covering them.*

The "garment" is an outward manifestation; in contrast, the "body" is the inner being. Of course, these are not bodies in a literal sense—not even in the sense of being independent entities.

In their essential nature, the *sefirot* themselves may be viewed as garments of the divine light that vivifies them, activates them, and gives them existence. However, since each *sefirah* has its own nature, we can speak of its "body"—that is, its defining character.

And they—

The *sefirot*.

Are called in this chapter—

Elijah's introduction uses the metaphor of the human body for the *sefirot*. Other chapters of the *Tikkunei Zohar* employ other symbols and terms as well. But those used here are the most common—in both the *Zohar* and other works of kabbalah—for they present the complete matrix of the "image of God."

Chesed *(lovingkindness)—*

That is the *sefirah* of flowing energy, giving, the desire to bestow.

Its inner being, its concealed nature, is the trait of love, which is the source of altruism, the desire to give—not to be rewarded, but out of an inner longing. More generally, the *sefirah* of *chesed* expresses expansion, outward movement from within, broadening and growth. Thus, this *sefirah* is also called *gedulah*, greatness or expansiveness and is symbolized by basic centrifugal movement, from the inside out. In the image of the human body it is represented by

The right arm,

Which typically is the active, working, and giving arm—as opposed to the left arm, which defends and receives.

Gevurah *(might)*—

This *sefirah* creates limitations. Fundamentally, it is ingathering, concentrating, centripetal. It is called *gevurah*, might, because in all of its manifestations—spiritual or physical—might is based upon the concentration of power.

It is also the trait of *din*, judgment, for it creates and sets limits, and is the source of precision in all matters.

In its inner being, it is fear, for the basic movement of fear is withdrawal and concealment.

In the human anatomy, this *sefirah* is represented by

The left arm.

This is the protective, passive arm, which acts primarily to assist, but does not display its own creative force.

Tiferet *(harmony).*

This is the *sefirah* of harmonious blending. In many senses, it is the locus of all the *sefirot*. As a central component of the *sefirotic* structure it contains within itself disparate elements (whether those are described in terms of intellect or emotion)—but these disparate elements share a common denominator and blend into one perfected being. The quality of this *sefirah* is therefore beauty, which is achieved principally by the correct proportion of color and shape.

In terms of emotion, the *sefirah* of *tiferet* is compassion. This is a combination of the loving and giving nature of *chesed* and the limitations of *gevurah*—in other words, the act of giving to those who deserve it.

In terms of awareness, it is the trait of truth, the mid-line, which does not veer to the side but penetrates to the essence.

In the image of the human body, it is represented by

The torso,

Which is the essence of the human structure, and which contains all of the vital inner organs.

The triad formed by these three *sefirot*—*chesed*, *gevurah*, and *tiferet*—is the archetypal structure of the *sefirot*: expansion, contraction, and integration. These three *sefirot* comprise a person's most basic feelings, from which, or through their combination, come the vast array of emotions.

In contrast, the next three *sefirot*—*netzach*, *hod*, and *yesod*—relate to the interface between the inner being and the outer world.

Netzach *and* hod *(victory and glory)*—

These two *sefirot* are described here, as in other texts, as one unit. Although they are separate entities, there is such a strong bond and similarity between them that they may be considered as two sides or aspects of the same being. Their shared characteristic is their resolute will to contain within themselves the inner traits of feeling and awareness, to foster them and to actualize them despite all barriers and obstacles from within and without.

The *sefirot* of *netzach* and *hod* express a forceful basic faithfulness. They express both belief and the will to hold on tenaciously. Yet, they also express the ability to break through barriers. *Netzach*, in the right-hand column, is the will to conquer and overcome obstacles; *hod*, in the left-hand column, is the ability to withstand the crushing weight of frustration.

In terms of the imagery of the human body, these two *sefirot* are represented by

The two legs.

This physical representation reflects their inner nature: a person's two legs work as one unit. Even though there are two legs, their function is practically the same, and the basic difference is that one is right and the other left. In addition, the principal function of the legs is not connected to the inner functions of the body. The legs are made to hold up the body and carry it from one place to another.

And yesod *(foundation)*—

The name of this *sefirah* comes from the verse, "The righteous man is an eternal foundation" (Proverbs 10:25) and therefore this *sefirah* is called *tzadik,* or righteous. This is because the structure of the next and final *sefirah, malchut,* as well as everything that comes about through *malchut,* derives from *yesod. Yesod* is the *sefirah* of connection and unimpeded current; it possesses the will and ability to transfer. This giving is not one-sided, but creates relationship and connectivity. The power of *yesod,* which is the desire to give generously, connects the *sefirot* above it with *malchut* below, like a pillar connecting heaven and earth. In the symbology of human anatomy, *yesod* is

> *The end of the torso,*

The reproductive organ, which expresses connection and giving in the act of reproduction. Its inner nature is the transmission from that which causes conception to that which is conceived. It is called "the completion of the torso," because in the *sefirotic* structure, it may be thought of as the final expression of *tiferet,* the "torso." Both *tiferet* and *yesod* are to be found on the central column. *Yesod* is the culmination of this column and its powers of integration.

The organ that represents *yesod* has sealed into it

> *The sign of the holy covenant:*

Circumcision. Here the concept of "covenant" is employed in a broad sense to indicate an inner unification of a variety of elements.

> *Malchut (kingship) is the mouth.*

Malchut is the final *sefirah*, the completion and culmination of the *sefirotic* structure. As such, it serves as a transforming station between the giving *sefirot* and the receiving universes below them. It is how the energy flow from above reaches down below.

Malchut has but one quality: the power of governance, the ability to affect matters lower than, and separated from, itself.

Alternatively, *malchut* may be thought of as speech, communication—the ability to express thoughts, awareness, and feelings. *Malchut* is the vessel that receives the energy from all the *sefirot* above it, and through which all of the *sefirot* express themselves in the subsequent universes.

When *malchut* is revealed in the world, it is called *Shechinah* ("indwelling"—usually referred to as "God's Presence"), for it is a divine illumination that dwells within the reality of the world; it is the inner life, the inner soul of all beings. (Specifically, we are here discussing *malchut* of *atzilut*, which makes the *sefirot* of the world of *atzilut* visible in the lower worlds of *beriah*, *yetzirah*, and *asiah*.)

Malchut is also called "*Knesset Yisrael*," the Congregation of Israel, for it gathers within its structure all the souls that come down to be revealed in the world. And the Bible and the sages refer to *malchut* by a great number of names and metaphors, as each name expresses a different illumination of the higher entities that shine within and through the divine indwelling.

In the human analogy, *malchut* is represented by the mouth as the organ of speech. Speech does not serve the body for its own sake, but is a means of expression; its words affect the reality outside the body. Similarly, *malchut* affects those levels below the *sefirot,* serving as an intermediary between the *sefirot* themselves and the other lower levels of reality.

> *It is called the oral Torah.*

The *sefirah* of *malchut* is identified with the revelation of the oral Torah. Unlike the written Torah, a revelation that, in essence, we do not understand, the oral Torah is accessible and comprehensible both in terms of intellectual knowledge and of teaching how to put that knowledge into action. The oral Torah is, therefore, a revelation from above that *malchut* reveals to human beings, below a revelation of the Indwelling Presence in the world.

Until this point, in addition to *malchut,* we have discussed the six *sefirot* that relate to the emotions as listed in the Bible: "Yours, God is the greatness [*chesed*] and the might [*gevurah*] and the beauty [*tiferet*] and the victory [*netzach*] and the glory [*hod*], for everything in the heavens and the earth [*yesod*]" (*Chronicles* I 29:11). At this point the *Zohar* turns to the higher *sefirot,* beginning with *chochmah* and *binah* and finally dealing with the highest *sefirah* of all, *keter.*

> Chochmah *(wisdom).*

This *sefirah* marks the beginning of revelation. It is like a blazing bolt of lightning that contains a complete and complex structure that is compressed with a single point. *Chochmah* is the initial seed of an idea. It does not develop linearly, but appears organically, as an entire image emerging from nothingness. In a human being, *chochmah* is the concentrated point, the initial kernel of insight. From *chochmah* flows all fundamental concepts, the basic objects of all consciousness. *Chochmah* is also the level of awareness that contains the seed of the ability to recognize truth.

Chochmah has an analogue in the human body, the brain,

That is inner thought.

Since it is not a broad and detailed thought, but an all-inclusive flash, it is not a thought that can be revealed and expressed—rather, it is a hidden awareness. Therefore, it is always intrinsically an inner thought.

Binah *(understanding).*

This is the *sefirah* of active, organized, and complex thought. *Binah* receives a basic concept, a latent idea, from *chochmah* and is the ability to grow and develop the seed of that idea, separating, defining, and rearranging it, creating new and more perfected structures. In *binah*, the primordial concept that came from *chochmah* is expanded (in an organized, conscious process) so that it becomes tangible. In the human body, *binah* is represented and

That is the heart.

In Biblical language, the heart is the seat of understanding and feeling.

With it, the heart understands.

This too is in keeping with the Biblical concept of the heart as the seat of conscious, structured thought. This phrase also implies emotion: since *binah* creates a broad structure of thought and reflection, it serves as a basis for emotions. The initial impulses of feeling are directed and given meaning in *binah*. *Binah* is "the understanding of the heart"—the conscious thought that attends every emotion. It hints to the way of understanding that is not only intellectual, but also the insight into feelings.

About these [Chochmah *and* binah] *two it is written,*

The hidden things are for the Lord our God"
(Deuteronomy *29:28*).

The *sefirot* that descend from *chesed* to *malchut* guide the world. Their activity may be discerned in all the worlds, because they are by nature turned outward, creating a bond between God and His worlds.

However, there is no direct way to connect with the divine *sefirot* of *chochmah* and *binah*, which are concerned solely with inner thought. Although they can be recognized in the world of action by the traces that they leave, *chochmah* and *binah* are completely removed from all worlds, just as a person's thoughts and feelings cannot be known by others but can only be inferred from his actions and words. Unlike the *sefirot* that are revealed through the ways of divine action in the world—"the revealed matters are for us and our children" (Deuteronomy ibid.)—the inner *sefirot, chochmah* and *binah*, are always "the hidden things for the Lord, our God."

Keter elyon *(supreme crown).*

That is the ultimate beginning, the essential will, which transcends *chochmah* and *binah. Keter* is the source from which everything streams. In it are all levels of being, even though it is itself Nothingness, an essence beyond all logic and reason, which no one can understand. The *Zohar* refers to *keter* as "the dark candle," a source radiating darkness: states of reality beyond access and comprehension. It is the great deep, the ultimate source from which the river flows.

That is keter malchut, *the crown of royalty.*

The beginning of existence, the essence of life ("with You is the source of life" [Psalms 36:10]), is to be found at the core of God's supreme will. This is called *keter malchut.*

In the imagery of the body, *keter* rides above the body, raising it to a higher level. The crown is the symbol of God's royalty—but in a more profound sense, the crown itself is His royalty. The beginning of every complete system—whether a universe or a human being—is called *keter* (crown). The end of every system is *malchut* (royalty). And in every system, *keter* functions as the *malchut* of a yet higher system. *Keter* is thus the meeting ground between God and the universes as well as between the universes themselves.

Within each universe, *keter* unifies all from beginning to end. *Keter* is the beginning of God's will, reaching to the ultimate goal, achieved through action and accomplishment within *malchut*. The ultimate purpose of God's will—*keter*—is thus found in *malchut*—"the final deed was first in thought" *Beriyah in Asiyah? Atzilut in Asiyah—? Sacred action*

> Of which the verse states: "From the very beginning,
> He tells the end" (Isaiah 46:10).

This expression sums up the entire scope of creation, including the role of God's will in determining its goal ("from the very beginning") to that goal's ultimate manifestation ("the end"). "He tells" (in the Hebrew, *maggid*) refers to more than speech or prediction—*maggid* is related to *naggad*, "drawing forth." God's will is drawn forth and proceeds from beginning to end, unifying beginning and end, *keter* and *malchut*. *Cause → Effect → Cause*

> It is the cranium of tefillin.

The cranium encases the brain and is used here as a metaphor, both positive and negative, for the sheer will that passes into reason or thought: this is *keter*, a sort of crown of the soul. The *tefillin* symbolize the brain and the powers of cognition and understanding that lie in the soul.

> Within—

The inner source, the inner light, within all ten *sefirot*,

Is the name MaH.

The inner source, the inner light, within all ten *sefirot*, is a divine name, the four letter name of God, the Tetragrammaton written in full—for example, the first letter (yud) is written not as one letter but as three letters that sound out and spell the word "yud": yud vav dalet. This name is the form in which one can write God's name in full when one converts the letters into the number system that the letters also represent. Gematria is the name of the system in which we view each letter as a number and can therefore add up the numerical equivalents of the letters that form each word. But because the vowels can be written in different ways, the numerical value of each way of writing is different. This holy name is written with the vowel Aleph and its numerical value is 45 (MaH). This name permeates the ten *sefirot* of the world of *atzilut*.

Which is the path of atzilut.

God's light spreads through the universe of *atzilut* via the divine name of MaH. *Atzilut* is the beginning of the "world of rectification"—the world that rectifies the primordial chaos and shattering of the vessels.

That shattering resulted from the energies emitted by the contraction of the divine name known as BN (an expansion of the Tetragrammaton into ten letters with the numerical value of 52).

MaH rectifies BN. The world of *atzilut* is the most perfect expression of the divine name MaH. Within other, lower worlds—*beriah*, *yetzirah*, and in particular *asiah*—this name is adulterated by the entities that it has come to rectify, with parts of earlier stages of reality, the era of the fallen "kings of chaos."

This irrigates the tree.

The tree represents the entire world of *atzilut*. The divine name MaH is the water that irrigates the tree and causes it to grow. In truth, this water irrigates all existence: not only the Tree of Life but the totality of all beings on all levels.

With its limbs and its branches.

In a simple, general sense, the *sefirot* of *atzilut* are arranged in the form of a descending line, from *chochmah* or *keter* to *malchut*.

Actually, however, the relationship between the *sefirot* is more complex, more like the model of the human body, with the torso as a middle column (*daat, tiferet, yesod*), the limbs as the *sefirot* of *chesed* and *gevurah* on the right and left respectively, and the branches of *netzach* and *hod* also on the right and left respectively. This complexity in the world of *atzilut* creates, further on, a complexity that goes beyond the simple architecture of the four archetypal worlds (*atzilut, beriah, yetzirah,* and *asiah*), but which includes complex, multibranched structures such as *heichalot* (palaces), *shvilim* (paths), and *netivim* (lanes) that branch out into many different sides.

Like water irrigating a tree, which grows because
of that irrigation.

This image comes to teach us that the divine flow of energy (the name MaH, the inner nature of *atzilut*) not only creates the Tree of Life but also maintains it and sustains its growth at every moment.

Master of the worlds, You are the Reason of reasons and the Cause of causes.

God is the "first cause" of reality. Everything that exists was created and is affected by another force to which it owes its being and motive power—but God is the beginning of all, the First Cause, the initial Source. God is preceded by nothing. God's Being is the ultimate beginning.

You irrigate the tree—

The world of *atzilut* and all of the created worlds.

With that flow—

Of life—the divine power on the level of the divine name MaH, streaming through and from *atzilut*.

That flow is like a soul to the body, giving the body life.

The divine power is the creator of the Tree of Life and it is that power that makes it grow and develop. And here Elijah adds: the divine power also gives the Tree of Life, its existence, its life force at every moment—a life source that is like the soul to the body. But we must also repeat and emphasize that, even though You are the Source of life and being, without Whom nothing could exist, and although all entities are like garments or means of expression of that inner One, none of them reflect Your true nature.

In You, there is no image or likeness.

You have no likeness or form, nor any point of comparison with or relationship to any imagery.

Although the prophets and sages describe the divine in terms of human, even physical imagery, those images relate to the way of revelation with the system of ten *sefirot* (paralleling the structure of man). This construct is used symbolically to reveal the divine in the Bible. But nothing, not even by way of analogy or illustration, pertains to the divine nature.

Of anything, inside—

Within the spiritual core of the worlds,

Or outside.

—within the revealed part of all the worlds.
In all of these, nothing reflects upon God Himself.

You created heaven and earth.

Just as You made the ten *sefirot*, supreme and nonmaterial essences, You also and correspondingly created the physical heavens and earth.

> *And You brought forth from them,*

From the heavens,
> *Sun, moon, stars and constellations.*
> *And upon the earth*

You brought forth

> *Trees, the Garden of Eden.*

The Garden of Eden is mentioned here as an earthly location blessed with an abundance of plants and animals coexisting in harmony.

> *Grasses, wild animals, beasts, birds, fish and human beings.*

All of these lower, physical beings exist so that

> *To know through them of the supreme beings.*

All beings of the lower spiritual echelons, whether in their general life patterns or as the particulars of their individual existences, are a reflection and extension of the highest entities. When we contemplate these lower beings, we can gain deep insights into those supreme spiritual entities we cannot view directly.

And how the upper and lower beings function.

All beings, whether heavenly forces or blades of grass, exhibit the patterns and structures of beings of yet higher universes. Someone who understands these patterns sees in them the encompassing laws that affect all strata of all universes.

And how the lower beings gain awareness of the higher beings.

When a person meditates upon the various creations of the world, when he sees and comprehensively understands the whole, he can become aware of a higher reality and of how God's energy descends from above. His knowledge of this world allows him to understand the upper worlds.

But no one knows You at all.

Despite all of the correspondences between upper and lower worlds, which make it possible for us to use our powers of imagination, inference, and insight to understand the upper realms, we know nothing of You.

And besides You, there is no Oneness, above and below.

You are the source of all existence and life. If the life force that streams from You were to cease its flow, everything would be an empty husk, a phantasm. You are the sole source of being and power. It is Your underlying force that connects upper worlds to lower worlds and one *sefirah* to another, maintaining the reality of all levels. This intertwined relationship on every level is due solely to the light of the Infinite One within them. The unification and connection between upper and lower, between one *sefirah* and another, is what sustains reality as it is. This connection, on all the levels, is only because of the Infinite Light that is found in them.

You are known—

To the worlds. However, You are not known as You truly are, but rather

As the Cause of all and the Master over all.

Every created entity senses that it has a Creator. Although the universes cannot know God as He truly is, they can know that there is a Cause. On a higher level, they know that there is a Master Who guides the universes.

Each sefirah *has a known name—*

Which is one of God's names. In addition to their own names (*chochmah*, *chesed*, etc.) and their other designations and symbols, the *sefirot* are associated with divine names. Each such name alludes to a revelation of divinity corresponding to a particular *sefirah*. For instance, one Holy Name corresponds to *chesed*, another to *gevurah*, and so forth.

This relationship between God's Names and the *sefirot* may be compared to the relationship between a shaft of light and a vessel into which it shines. The light does not change. What does change is the effect that light has, the color it takes on, as it shines through the vessel. Similarly, the light of the Infinite One shines on all the universes only through the *sefirot*.

By which the angels are called.

The names of the angels come from the names of the *sefirot* (or *heichalot*) with which they are associated—for example, Gabriel comes from *gevurah*. Each angel receives its power and personality from its particular *sefirah*, and its mission corresponds to the nature of that *sefirah*.

But You have no known name.

An angel has the name that corresponds to its *sefirah* and the *sefirah* has the name that relates to its characteristic activity. But for You, no state of being, no name, can define You.

The names of God that appear in the Bible and Talmud are not His names as He truly is. They are a description, rather, of the divine revelation in a particular manner, in a particular *sefirah*. All that we can say about God's "great name" is that it cannot be revealed or known. That name preceded the existence of all the universes—"before the world was created, the Holy One, blessed be He, and His Name alone existed" (Pirkei Derabbi Eliezer 3)—and it rises higher than any reality—"His name alone is exalted" (Psalms 148:13). Like God Himself, His name transcends all being and comprehension. Like the infinite divine light, God's name cannot be apprehended—all we can perceive is its glory and radiance as they shine upon the heavens and earth.

For You fill all names.

None of the names of God that are knowable to us are identified with God's utmost Being. You are the inner core of those names. They are no more than designations of "garments" and framework.

And You are the wholeness of all.

Your wholeness, even though it is beyond existence, includes every type of completeness.

All created states of being are, by definition, lacking and imperfect. But You, the uncreated Creator, the Holy One Who brings all into being, the true and sole Infinite One, You are the supreme perfection that perfects all. *Rectification*

When You leave them, all of the names
remain like a body without a soul.

These divine names are not independent entities. If they have no more connection to, if they are no longer nurtured by, their source, they cannot continue to exist and act. If the divine light absents itself, these divine names can no longer remain as they had been—just as a word only has the meaning in relation to the reality which it describes.

You are wise.

The Bible refers to God as wise (e.g., Isaiah 31:2 and *Targum Yonatan* there).

But not with a known wisdom.

Although God is described as wise, that is merely a description of how He acts (just as we refer to Him as "causing the wind to blow and the rain to descend"). Ordinary wisdom has no relationship to God's infinite, essential Being, for it is a limited and self-enclosed quality. "The wisdom of God" is a wisdom that we cannot comprehend, a wisdom that can be compared to no other.

You are understanding.

This description too may be found in the Bible (Psalms 33:15; Chronicles I 38:9).

But not with a known understanding.

Our minds cannot grasp God's understanding nor any of His other supreme traits.

You have no known place.

It is true that we use expressions such as "blessed is the glory of G-d from His place" (prayer book; cf. Ezekiel 3:12), but this simply means, "wherever His Presence is revealed." We surely do not mean a place in the physical sense of the word. The physical sense cannot be seen to relate to any definition of place, even in the most abstract sense. We cannot attribute any physicality to God, not even in the most rarified sense.

But in order to make Your power and
might known to human beings,

We have no way of knowing Your essential Being, for we can know You only by Your actions. Your divine revelation is expressed through the *sefirot.*

And to show them how the world
is guided with judgment and compassion.

This is another reason God reveals Himself through the *sefirot*: so that we can gain an appreciation of divine providence. At times, the trait of judgment creates punishment and difficulties for certain individuals. At other times, situations are suffused by compassion, the divine protection against evil, and a wealth of blessing.

For there exist justice and lawfulness—

In the world. Events do not occur by happenstance. Rather,

In accordance with the deeds of human beings.

Man's deeds are not meaningless, nor are they without conse-quence. Good behavior is rewarded and evil is punished.

God's revelation cannot only resonate to His transcendent comprehension. In order to understand reward and punish-ment, we require a revelation that relates to the finite, for that reality makes it possible for us to find meaning in the revela-tion. Thus, the avenues of revelation must be mediated through the *sefirot*. As filtering mechanisms, the *sefirot* bring these ener-gies down from level to level until they reach our world (on both its spiritual and physical levels), where we can understand them as reward and punishment. These *sefirotic* mechanisms, or traits, whose energies guide our world, do not express the essen-tial divine Being, but only the manner in which God reveals Himself through them.

The following expresses the avenues of revelation.

Judgment corresponds to [the sefirah*] of* gevurah.

The phrases "the judgment of heaven" and "the trait of judg-ment" refer to the *sefirah* of *gevurah*.

Lawfulness corresponds to the middle column.

Lawfulness is a reference to *tiferet*, the trait of compassion, which is in a sense the locus of all the *sefirot*, residing in the cen-ter of the middle column.

Exacting justice corresponds to holy malchut.

Exacting justice is total and uncompromising, without taking into account the circumstances and difficulties of the person being judged. Holy *malchut* is severe judgment. (It corresponds to the divine name Adnut.) Next, we come to:

The just scales (cf. Leviticus 19:36).

These "just scales" are the *sefirot* of *netzach, hod,* and *yesod,* which make use of *malchut* to perform the operation of exacting justice: weighing facts with complete impartiality, not bending to either side. These three *sefirot* may be divided into two units. The first is referred to as:

Two pillars of truth.

These are the two *sefirot* of *netzach* and *hod,* which stand side by side, in the right and left-hand columns respectively, balanced like scales, together with

A just measure (Leviticus 19:36).

That is *yesod.* As for *yesod,*

That is the sign of the holy covenant.
All of this,

The way that the world is guided through the medium of the *sefirot* has a sole purpose: it is

To demonstrate—

In a clear and comprehensible manner

How the world functions. But not that You have—

These traits. You, yourself, do not have these traits in Your essential Being. These words are meaningless when it comes to You.

A known [trait of] exacting justice, which is judgment.

Although, as we saw earlier, exacting justice is associated with *malchut*; here it is also connected with judgment, which is *gevurah*. (The *sefirot* may be arranged in a two-column configuration. *Malchut* is then in the left-hand column, as is *gevurah*.)

Exacting justice requires judgment, for it involves determining the application of the law, without compromise.

Nor a known lawfulness, which is [associated with] compassion.

Lawfulness carries a somewhat different connotation than judgment. Unlike justice, which is pure, strict judgment, lawfulness takes into account factors that can ameliorate the strict judgment.

Lawfulness is thus characteristic of *tiferet*, the trait of compassion, the nuanced blending of *chesed* and *gevurah*.

Nor any of these measures—

That is to say, the names that correspond to the *sefirot*, describing God as Loving, Mighty, Gracious, Merciful, Righteous and King.

Whatsoever.

God Himself has no relationship to these traits. They are merely descriptions of how He acts in His universes.

"Blessed be God forever, amen and amen" (Psalms 89:53).

Elijah closes with a verse that praises God and is also the source of what was said above.

This verse is understood, according to kabbalah, as an expression of the descent and flow of the supreme abundance, the Abstract and the Infinite, into the boundaries of the world. The word "blessed" indicates how divine energy is drawn down; The Hebrew name Lord here is the great name of God that precedes all being, and that is drawn down into "the world."

In this essay, Elijah has dealt with the drawing forth and descent of the infinite, indefinable, and incomprehensible light into boundaries and vessels, where God reveals Himself and acts within the universes. These vessels are the ten *sefirot* whose essence is the relationship among the *sefirot* and the relationship of the *sefirot* to God, which are the themes of this chapter.